The Religious Journey

THE EXISTENCE OF GOD

Randall K. Stewart

Randy Stewart
6-27-05

Note for Librarians: a cataloguing record for this book that includes Dewey Decimal Classification and US Library of Congress numbers is available from the Library and Archives of Canada. The complete cataloguing record can be obtained from their online database at:
www.collectionscanada.ca/amicus/index-e.html
ISBN 1-4120-5110-X
Printed in Victoria, BC, Canada

Printed on paper with minimum 30% recycled fibre. Trafford's print shop runs on "green energy" from solar, wind and other environmentally-friendly power sources.

TRAFFORD

Offices in Canada, USA, Ireland and UK
This book was published *on-demand* in cooperation with Trafford Publishing. On-demand publishing is a unique process and service of making a book available for retail sale to the public taking advantage of on-demand manufacturing and Internet marketing. On-demand publishing includes promotions, retail sales, manufacturing, order fulfilment, accounting and collecting royalties on behalf of the author.

Book sales for North America and international:
Trafford Publishing, 6E–2333 Government St.,
Victoria, BC v8t 4p4 CANADA
phone 250 383 6864 (toll-free 1 888 232 4444)
fax 250 383 6804; email to orders@trafford.com
Book sales in Europe:
Trafford Publishing (uk) Ltd., Enterprise House, Wistaston Road Business Centre,
Wistaston Road, Crewe, Cheshire cw2 7rp UNITED KINGDOM
phone 01270 251 396 (local rate 0845 230 9601)
facsimile 01270 254 983; orders.uk@trafford.com
Order online at:
trafford.com/05-0004

10 9 8 7 6 5 4

To Clarence and Mary Lou Stewart,
my parents,
who informed me as a baby of God's existence,
embraced me as a child when my heart believed,
encouraged me as an adult when my mind doubted,
rejoice with me today that heart and mind are one.
There is no way I could repay my debt to you.

FOREWORD

In his well-known autobiography *Surprised by Joy*, C. S. Lewis relates that before he experienced conversion to Christian faith, he experienced conversion of another sort, a more radical sort actually–he became convinced of the existence of God. He became, in short, a theist, rather than an atheist (which he pretended for a while to be) or an agnostic (a position he found more defensible intellectually, but no more satisfying).

Lewis resisted this conversion to theism, not least because he realized that, alas, if it were really true, that if anything like the God of the Christians really existed, then his life would change forever. "Amiable agnostics will talk cheerfully about 'man's search for God,'" Lewis recalled, but "[t]o me, as I then was, they might as well have talked about the mouse's search for the cat."[1]

Lewis' experience perhaps explains why philosophers and theologians over the centuries have spilt so much ink on arguments for and against the existence of God. God certainly has more to do than merely to exist, as George MacDonald somewhere said, but if such a Being does exist, the implications are immeasurably immense. Anyone might glibly answer a pollster's question about belief in God–ninety percent plus of Americans say "yes" every year–but no one can truly confront the reality that (as Francis Schaeffer phrased it) "He is there," and take it lightly.

For that very reason, Dr. Randy Stewart's *Religious Journey* is, in a manner of speaking, *dangerous*. Like the scholars, Dr. Stewart has examined, thoroughly examined, the evidences for belief in God. But more importantly, like Lewis, he has come to grips with the disturbing consequences of believing–or not believing. And now, most disturbingly, he invites you to come to grips with God yourself.

---

[1] C.S. Lewis, *Inspired by Joy: The Shape of My Early Life* (New York: Harcourt Brace Jovanovich, 1955), 227.

He is your guide through the "whether" of God's existence, and he is your companion through the "so what?"

As to the "whether," Dr. Stewart is a skillful guide indeed. He presents complex ideas in easily digestible form. His writing proves the point of Professor Stephen Evans, whom he quotes (Day 12), that "Belief in God is genuinely coherent with all we know about ourselves and our universe."

As to the "so what?," Dr. Stewart has passed this "dangerous" road himself and found that it leads at last to a heavenly court. It may feel in the beginning like "the mouse's search for the cat," but it ends in a room full of Brie.

A thousand years before Jesus Christ, and three thousand before C. S. Lewis or Randy Stewart, King David declared, "The fool has said in his heart, 'There is no God'" (Ps. 14.1). If God is there, and we deny Him, we are fools. But what should we call ourselves if we never bother to ask the question?

C. Richard Wells

C. Richard Wells, past president and professor of Pastoral Theology at The Criswell College in Dallas, Texas, today serves as the senior pastor of South Canyon Baptist Church in Rapid City, South Dakota.

INTRODUCTION

Why would an emergency physician choose to write about the existence of God, and why should I choose to read what he says? These are the first two questions that may enter your mind when you pick up this book, and they are the very questions I want to address in this introduction.

I was a "seminary baby," born in 1956 in Louisville, Kentucky while my father was preparing for the pastorate. It is not an exaggeration to say that my formative years revolved around the church and that I developed at an early age an appetite for all things religious. Before I could read or write, I could sing all the familiar hymns by memory, even the oft-ignored third verses. I can remember reciting in order the sixty-six books of the Bible before I could name the fifty states. I would read children's Bible story collections from cover to cover, then read them over again. By the age of seven, I knew enough about the Christian faith to genuinely realize my need for repentance and conversion. I became a Christian then (to this day, I have no doubt that I knew what I was doing) and was baptized into the fellowship of the Church.

Unlike many of my peers, my teenage years were marked by obedience to my parents. I never did "sow my wild oats," electing instead to keep my life pretty much "between the white lines." All the while, I kept accumulating knowledge–all of it in a conservative, Southern Baptist format–about God and the Bible. By the time I graduated from high school, I can honestly say that I knew more Bible facts than any person I had met who was my age and more than most who were several years my senior.

It is not surprising, then, that I left home for college in 1974 fully intending to become the fifth minister to dot the family tree. (In addition to my father, my maternal grandfather and two of my uncles were pastors.) I quickly declared religion as my major, to which I later added history as a second major. My beliefs at the time of my enrollment were largely a reflection of my exposure as a child. I believed in God almost as a reflex, never entertaining the possibility that He might not exist. My view of the Bible was typical of most mainstream Southern Baptists–conservative, without any trace of leftward leanings. As is true of many conservatives, I knew what I believed and never questioned why I believed it. Unaware of its shaky subjective foundation, I considered my faith to be rock-solid.

This all changed in a period of three months the fall of my sophomore year. It was then that I first became aware of a galaxy of thought much different than my own. I studied in one class history's greatest philosophers, many of them atheists, and found their incessant questions about life and God unsettling. In another class, I read the works of theologians whose views of the Bible seemed slanted in a moderate-to-liberal direction. I remember being excited about exploring these new horizons but, at the same time, apprehensive about their potential to shake my belief system at its very core. I listened to fellow students, most of them upper-classmen, who in typical cocksure fashion poked fun at anyone within the narrow confines of traditional belief. To say the least, it was a time of soul-searching and introspection, the first time I remember doubt and my faith mentioned in the same breath.

I am not implying that all I experienced that sophomore year was negative. In fact, I embrace today many views about God and the Bible that were introduced to me then. The problem for me was not so much that I faced new ideas but that they were thrust upon me in a short period of time in such volume. Much like a novice rider on a powerful motorcycle, I was being asked to control more than I could safely handle. As would be expected, given the implications thereof, the arguments I heard against God's existence troubled me the most. The men and women espousing them seemed to be so educated and so passionate in their defenses. They appeared to have so much to say and could say it with certainty and flare. I, on the other hand, had no immediate answers. My college professors helped a great deal by presenting counter-arguments to the atheists, but these rebuttals were new to me and not yet internalized by me. It would take a while–years, in fact–for them to take root. All the while, my ship of faith, continuously rocked by waves of doubt, began to show signs of wear and tear.

While this intellectual struggle raged within me, I continued on a practical level to live as if God's existence was certain. No one who observed me on a casual basis would have imagined me to be in any degree of perplexity. Only my closest college friends, with whom I shared my questions and doubts, knew what was going on. They knew the rest of the story, that I was being forced to reevaluate everything I had been told as a child and had accepted "hook, line, and sinker." Such second-hand, subjective belief was no longer enough for me. I needed an objective foundation for my faith and began to search in earnest for it.

This curious admixture of faith and doubt colored all the major decisions I made in the next few years. If someone had looked close enough for long enough, my internal dichotomy would have been evident. I finished my studies in religion and history, graduated with honors from college, visited seminary as a prospective student, then shunned the ministry in favor of the pursuit of medicine. In light of my wavering theology, I envisioned some difficulties in the future standing before a congregation whose basic beliefs were different and, worse yet, more secure than my own. I began to feel out of step with my denomination, and I feared covert or open reprisals from the convention hierarchy if my convictions turned out to be too "unconventional." So I opted for pre-medical instead of pre-ministerial studies, medical school instead of seminary, a Doctor of Medicine instead of a Doctor of Ministry degree. And I remained the consummate paradox, serving as minister of music at a small suburban church to help pay medical school expenses in an attempt to avoid the ministry altogether.

As is so often true in times of theological upheaval, subtle cracks began to form in my character. My moral fiber began to have frayed edges, as slowly and almost imperceptibly the relativism of the day pervaded my thoughts and actions. The lines separating right and wrong became blurred and indistinct, which produced in me something good (a tolerance of others that I sorely lacked in my conservative days) and something not so good (a tendency to rationalize my behavior). Gradually over several years, I saw key relationships in my life deteriorate due to neglect or injury on my part. I was not as moral on the outside as I once was, even less so on the inside. Although stopping shy of outright rebellion against the morality of my youth, I detoured enough that those closest to me could notice the change and enough that I could consider myself to be every bit of the hypocrite.

Fortunately, I never gave up on faith. I kept searching for answers to my questions. As time would allow, I read defenses of theism by some of the greatest apologists, past and present. I understood most of their arguments and, after rejecting a few that seemed to me a little strained, accepted the majority as true. I listened to their brilliant analogies and illustrations, internalized them, and added to them some of my own. In time, I became one who found myself nodding in agreement with them. I found myself more and more solidly in the camp of theism, not just because of pedigree or emotion but also because of objectivity and reason. I came to fully believe in God once again because I discovered that the universe in which I lived made the most sense if He existed. I maintain that same faith today, a faith that has met doubt head-on and, while not eliminating it entirely, has rendered it meaningless. Although my belief in God may not be as dogmatic as in my youth, it is a conviction with deeper roots and is today a source of genuine happiness and peace. This alone has made my religious journey worthwhile.

What you are about to read is that religious pilgrimage recounted in summary form. It is written with full acknowledgment of my limitations as a writer and theologian but with the sincere hope that my God-given gifts of simplification, analogy, and organization

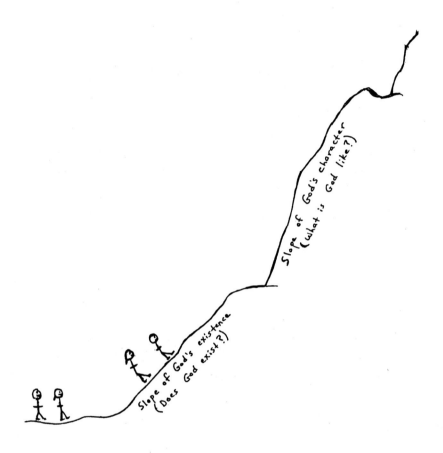

Figure 1:
The Religious Journey Begins

Day 1
the universal starting point

"If we refuse to discuss the existence of God, we are simply avoiding the central issue..."

- philosopher ELTON TRUEBLOOD

The initial destination for all religious seekers is the existence of God. No matter how high they may eventually climb in their individual pilgrimages or what paths they may take to get there, their first few steps must always be the same. They all must ascend the slope of God's existence before proceeding any further. Only then can their religious quests continue in earnest. If there is no God, to forge ahead would be foolish.[1]

The vast majority of men and women throughout history who have stood at the foot of that mountain and taken these initial steps has come to the conclusion that God does exist. Some have restricted their worship to one God, as seen in the three great monotheistic religions: Judaism, Christianity, and Islam. Others have embraced a plethora of gods, Hindu polytheism being a prime example. But never is there religion without some type of god in the spotlight. A religion without a god would be like a water molecule without hydrogen, meaningless and impossible.

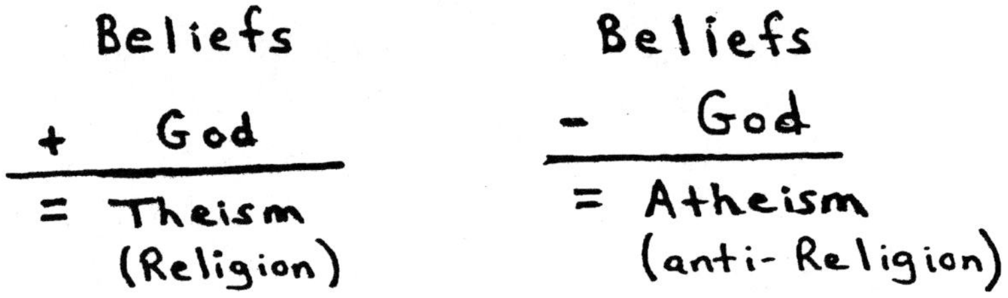

$$\begin{array}{r} \text{Beliefs} \\ + \quad \text{God} \\ \hline = \text{Theism} \\ \text{(Religion)} \end{array} \qquad \begin{array}{r} \text{Beliefs} \\ - \quad \text{God} \\ \hline = \text{Atheism} \\ \text{(anti-Religion)} \end{array}$$

Figure 2:

Theism and Atheism Contrasted

Day 2
religion and atheism contrasted

*"I am an atheist and this means at least: I do not believe
there is a god, or any gods, personal or in nature, or
manifesting himself, herself, or itself in any way."*

- atheist MADALYN MURRAY O'HAIR

Some would argue that atheism, a belief system denying the existence of God, is as much a religion as all the others. Here I would beg to differ. All religions have in common a group of people who acknowledge, perceive, and reverence a Reality (or group of realities) considered divine and who do so to a point that influences their day-to-day activities. Atheists, on the other hand, have ceased to look to any divine source for truth. They believe that no spiritual dimension exists that can affect their lives on a daily basis. For this reason, atheism is not in any sense a religion. In fact, it is just the opposite. It is anti-religion, life lived without a divine impulse.

I am aware that some people today define religion in such a way that atheism could be included therein. The difference in their definition and mine is mainly one of semantics. They define religion as any system of beliefs, any worldview. I limit it to those belief systems that include the worship of God or the supernatural. That is why atheism is not, in my opinion, a religion. Inside its shell of beliefs it has no spiritual core. It is, admittedly, a belief system, but it is one that is separate from and antithetical to religion itself.[1]

Figure 3:
One Advantage of Theism

Day 3
advantage #1 of theism: life after death

The Dogma of Atheism
There is no God.
There is no objective truth.
There is no ground for reason.
There are no absolute morals.
There is no ultimate value.
There is no ultimate meaning.
There is no eternal hope.

- apologist STEVE KUMAR

It matters much whether or not a person believes in the existence of God. If there is no God, reality is confined entirely to the natural world, to this universe. There is nothing "out there," nothing above or beyond nature, nothing supernatural or (described more accurately) *supra*-natural to acknowledge or with which to interact. One's life in such a universe would have no spiritual or supernatural component. It would arise out of nature and in the end be reabsorbed into nature, much like a drop of water is recollected into the ocean. There would be no life after death, in the sense most of us tend to think about it, for death would signal a return of our physical components to nature to be recycled as nature would dictate. This earthly life would be all there is, a life without eternal hope, one that lives on only through the legacy it leaves behind. Contrast this with the person who believes in God. He or she acknowledges a Reality that is more than the physical world, a spiritual dimension that is just as real as nature, and an eternal hope that his or her spirit will continue after death has destroyed the flesh.

This is the biggest difference, as I see it, between atheism and theism, and it is no small matter. If you doubt its importance, just ask one hundred people on death's doorstep whether they wish to continue as a distinct individual or merely be absorbed into nature.

It would be the rare individual who would choose the latter. Then ask one hundred mothers and fathers whose children have died before them if it matters whether or not they will some day interact with their son or daughter in a personal way. I cannot fathom one parent who would not immediately and joyously embrace the prospect of such a reunion.

In short, no relationship beyond death is even remotely conceivable to the atheist. Theism alone permits this blessed hope.[1]

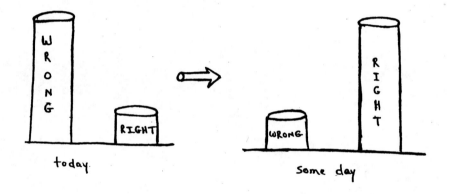

Figure 4:
Another Advantage of Theism

Day 4
advantage #2 of theism: justice for all

> *"My father and mother were deeply religious. My brother and I had no time for religion... Then my brother was killed. My father and mother had resources, and with their resources they could meet that shattering loss. But I had no one. I had no resources at all."*

> - scientist ROBERT J. DEAN

Another benefit of theism over atheism is that only in the former can justice prevail. Almost every person on this earth, it seems, has a sense of justice. If we play a board game, we want it to be played fairly. If we seek a promotion, we want fair and equitable treatment. If the game or the hiring isn't fair, there is something that innately recoils within us, something that desires the wrong to be made right.

The frustrating fact is that all of us, so universally bent on fairness, live in a world that at times seems so unfair. Hear the psalmist, complaining to God that the righteous suffer and the wicked prosper.[1] Listen to Job, demanding a day in court with God to address his undeserved treatment.[2] Recall the words of Jesus, asking "why?" as he hung in torture on the cross.[3] They are professing what we all know to be true, that the world is not a fair place and that, in this life only, there is virtually no hope that justice will prevail.

Whether standing beside an innocent sufferer's bedside or observing on television tragedies abroad, I too cannot help but sense the unfairness of life and also sense, while longing for justice, that it will be incomplete if it comes at all. I cannot make all things right, and neither can you. Although I believe that we should do our part whenever possible to right wrongs in this world, I know that our collective efforts will always fall short of utopia. Unless God intervenes, we will never live "happily ever after."

This is the final conclusion of atheism, the end of the story. It proclaims that belief in God is only "make-believe." Consequently, when it sees we inhabit a universe that does not treat us fairly, it foresees that this will forever be the case. Then it advises us to resign ourselves to this pessimism and move ahead. It asks us to quit looking for ultimate justice, for ultimate justice is not possible in the random, mechanical, impersonal universe it perceives.[4]

Contrast this with theism. It allows its adherents to entertain the possibility of eventual justice (if not in this life, then in the life beyond), because it asserts that there is more to the universe than nature itself. If this supernatural Reality values justice, it assures us that we have every reason to hope that justice will someday come.

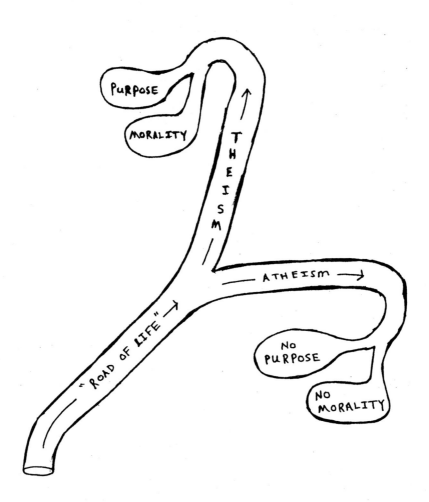

Figure 5:

Two More Advantages of Theism

Day 5
advantages #3 and #4: absolute morality and true purpose

"If God does not exist, we find no values or commands to turn to which legitimize our conduct."

- atheist JEAN-PAUL SARTRE

Life is "… a tale told by an idiot, full of sound and fury, signifying nothing."

- playwright WILLIAM SHAKESPEARE

Apologists often cite two additional disadvantages of atheism. The first is that it gives us an amoral universe with no possibility of moral absolutes, and the second is that it presents to us a purposeless universe with no possibility of individual or community purpose.

While I understand these arguments and basically agree with them, they are not as helpful to me as the two I have already proposed. If I were an atheist, I can imagine myself, even in an amoral world, living what appears to be a "moral" life. Whether I did so because of natural instincts and genetic tendencies or because I wanted to strive for the common good in this world, I can see myself and other atheists behaving as fairly decent individuals, appearing in every respect to be "moral" and "upright." I also can easily imagine, even if I believed in a purposeless world, having what appears to be a worthy purpose or goal for my life. I think I would want to live in a manner that would positively impact those around me and secure for myself a meaningful legacy. If this is not purpose, it's something very close to it.

Thus, while only a belief in God allows the possibility of absolute morality and true purpose, atheism permits at least the appearance of a moral and purposeful life. That is why these last two advantages of theism do not resonate with me as loudly as the others. When it comes to a personal life after death and eventual justice for all, however, it is an entirely different matter. The atheist has nothing at all to offer and the theist everything. On these two points, an honest atheist must concede to the theist complete and total advantage.

KNOW GOD...

   ... KNOW ETERNAL LIFE

   ... KNOW EVENTUAL JUSTICE

NO GOD...

   ... NO ETERNAL LIFE

   ... NO EVENTUAL JUSTICE

Figure 6:
**Bumper Stickers
of the Theist (above)
and Atheist (below)**

Day 6
the task before us

"...no fire, no heroism, no intensity of thought and feeling can preserve an individual life beyond the grave... all the labour of the ages, all the devotion, all inspiration, all the noonday brightness of human genious, are destined to extinction in the vast death of the solar system... the whole temple of Man's achievement must inevitably be buried beneath the debris of a universe in ruins."

— agnostic BERTRAND RUSSELL

The atheist, therefore, cannot conceive of a personal life after death, nor can he hope for all things unjust to one day be made right. Only the theist can see these as possibilities. This seeming advantage of the theist over the atheist becomes meaningless, however, if the atheist is right and the theist wrong about the existence of God. If the atheist is right, then the theist's dream of life after death and justice for all is a mirage and should be quickly abandoned. Only if the atheist is wrong—if God, indeed, does exist—can you or I entertain the possibility of living beyond death and seeing justice prevail.

God's existence, then, is the first hurdle we must leap in our religious quest. Only then can we determine if we have any reason to hope at all. Only then, when we truly believe He does exist, can we begin to look at His character. Only after perceiving His character can we begin to see whether or not our hopes are in vain.

The task before us can be simply stated: we must first examine the existence of God to see if eternal hope is possible and, if so confirmed, must then examine His nature and character to see if this hope is reasonable.[1]

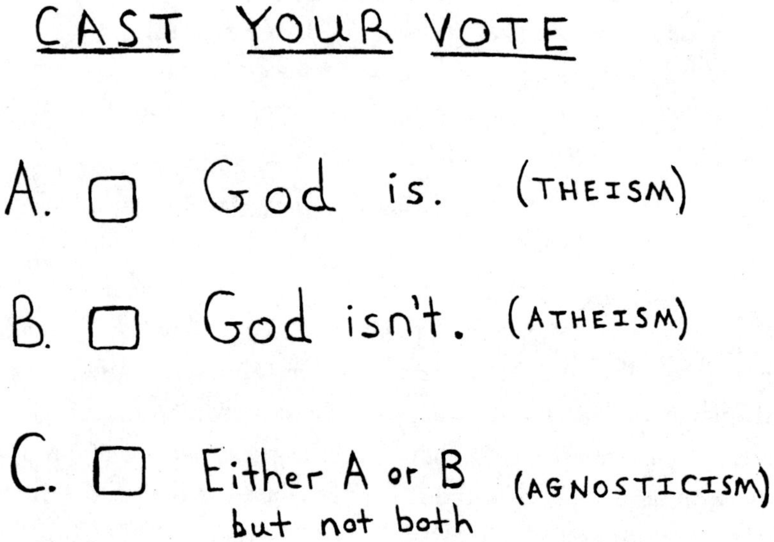

CAST YOUR VOTE

A. ☐ God is. (THEISM)

B. ☐ God isn't. (ATHEISM)

C. ☐ Either A or B (AGNOSTICISM)
        but not both

Figure 7:
The Religious Ballot

Day 7
God's existence: the two possibilities

"The question whether there is or is not a god can and should be rewarding, in that it can yield definite results."

- Oxford atheistic philosopher J. L. MACKIE

Either God exists or He does not; there are no other possibilities.

The theist asserts that the former is true, that there is a supernatural, divine force behind the universe. The atheist believes the latter, that there is no God and that any such notion is but a myth.

That only one of these two is correct can be easily surmised by common sense. If God exists, as the theist asserts, then the atheist cannot be right to any degree. If the atheist is right and there is no God, then the theist is 100% wrong. There is no middle ground. Even the agnostic, who cannot decide whether or not God exists, would agree that only one or the other (certainly not both) is true.

Regarding the reality of God, therefore, our discussion is limited to two possibilities: either God exists or He does not.[1]

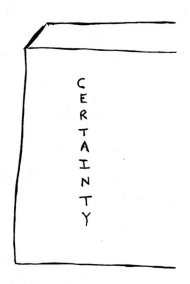

ARGUMENTS FOR AND AGAINST THE EXISTENCE OF GOD

CERTAINTY

Figure 8:
**The Limitations of
Theological Arguments**

Day 8
the limitations of theological arguments

*"Those who believe they believe in God but without
passion in the heart, without anguish of mind,
without uncertainty, without doubt, and even at
times without despair, believe only in the idea
of God, and not in God Himself."*

- Christian MADELEINE L'ENGLE

Theists most likely will never be able to prove God's existence, if by "proof" we mean certainty beyond any doubt. Their arguments may be reasonable, rational, and logical, but they will never be absolute. Although they may appeal to common sense, they will always end at a point shy of complete certainty, leaving faith (based on the evidence at hand) as the final bridge to belief.

The irony, however, is that atheists cannot prove their position either. They, too, use rational arguments to support their beliefs, but their arguments likewise yield an inevitable degree of dubiety. They do not possess a monopoly on certitude any more than do the theists.

In short, neither the theist nor the atheist can prove beyond any doubt that God exists or does not.[1]

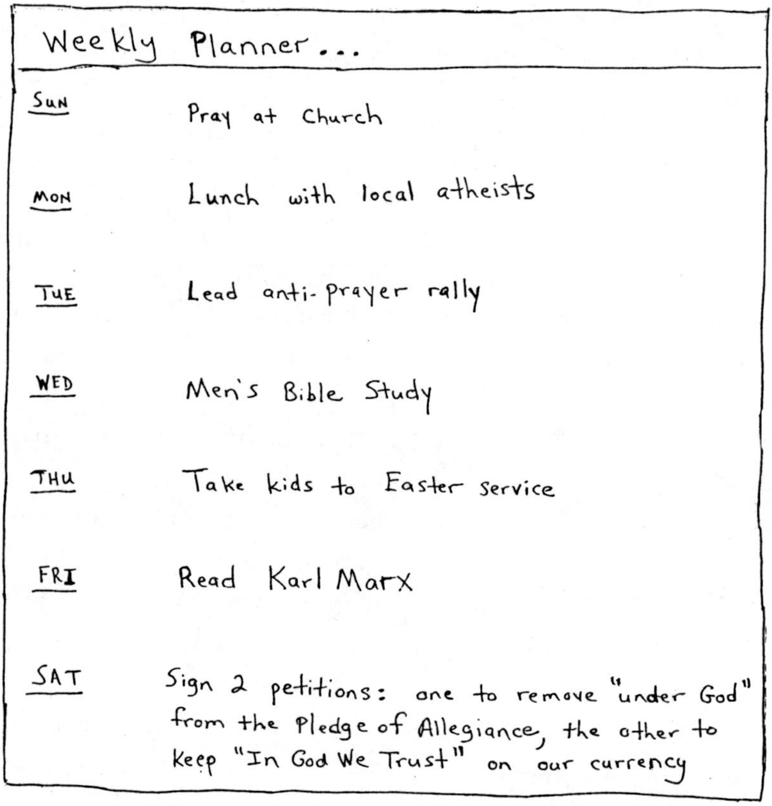

Weekly Planner...

SUN	Pray at Church
MON	Lunch with local atheists
TUE	Lead anti-prayer rally
WED	Men's Bible Study
THU	Take kids to Easter service
FRI	Read Karl Marx
SAT	Sign 2 petitions: one to remove "under God" from the Pledge of Allegiance, the other to keep "In God We Trust" on our currency

Figure 9:

Agnosticism – Practical Nonsense

Day 9
the impracticality of agnosticism (I)

"The conclusion we reach in our reflection on this question [Does God exist?] has the most momentous consequences in the orientation of our thinking and of our daily living."

- philosopher EDWARD SILLEM

If neither theists nor atheists can absolutely defend their positions, why shouldn't we all face this realization honestly and resign ourselves to agnosticism? Shouldn't we all shake hands and agree that it's impossible to know whether or not God exists? Wouldn't that be the best and most practical solution? My answer is "no," and let me try to explain why.

Intellectually, I have to agree that there is some truth to this line of thinking. If I am honest, I must admit as a theist that my thought processes have fallen short of proving God exists. I may be 90% sure intellectually, but that leaves 10% doubt. The honest atheist would admit the same, that there lurks in his or her mind a degree of uncertainty, unreachable by logical arguments. I guess you could say, intellectually speaking, that both the theist and the atheist have a little bit of the agnostic in them and will always have.

That would be the end of the whole matter if we all lived in a world strictly intellectual, one confined to our thoughts alone. This, of course, is not the case. Our existence consists of action as well as thought, and this very activity makes it impossible to embrace agnosticism as a practical alternative. It would be maddening, in fact, to conduct my life consistent with my intellectual dichotomy. My life would be inconsistent at best if I determined to spend 90% of my waking hours as if God existed and 10% as if He didn't. The atheist would have the same problem if 10% of his or her actions turned out to be religious. Such an existence would be unacceptable to us all and would be decried as the height of hypocrisy.

My point here is that agnosticism, although in some respects the only intellectual alternative, cannot be lived in practice. In fact, it amounts to practical nonsense. The sensible thing for the agnostic would be to weigh his or her doubts in the balance, pick the most likely intellectual position, and then live as if that position were 100% correct. It would be best if he or she would become a practicing theist or atheist. But then, on a practical level, he or she would cease to be an agnostic altogether.

Such is the problem with agnosticism. It is intellectually acceptable but pragmatically infeasible. It is a mental exercise with little or no practical value.

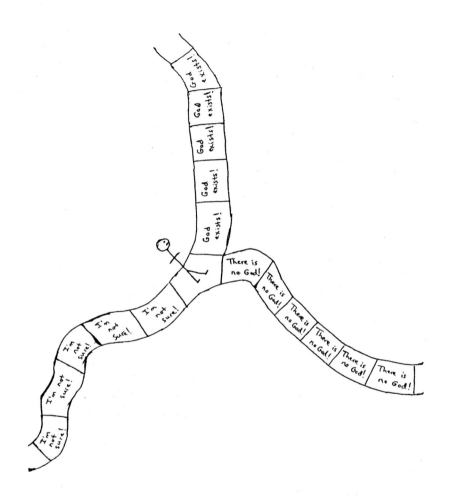

Figure 10:
The Agnostic's Practical Dilemma

Day 10
the impracticality of agnosticism (II)

"I do not pretend to be able to prove that there is no God."

- agnostic BERTRAND RUSSELL

An illustration may serve to drive home the fallacy of agnosticism:

Suppose that a seven-year-old girl arrives home from school and tells her father that her teacher has questioned her belief in a moon made of cheese. He asks her what she believes now, and she replies, "I'm not sure if I believe her or not. I'm just confused right now about the whole thing." It would be very possible for this girl to continue to hold these two opposing thoughts in her mind for some time without any charge of inconsistency being leveled at her, because she does not have to act upon either of these thoughts. Not one of her daily activities is influenced or affected by her position on the cholesterol content of the moon. To her, this is 100% an intellectual dilemma. It has 0% practical value.

Suppose again that the next day she returns saying her teacher does not believe in a real Santa Claus and that she again tells her father she has not yet made up her mind if this is true. Now she has a real problem when Christmas rolls around. She may be 50% certain that Santa Claus exists and 50% certain that he does not, but it is impossible for her to be that ambiguous in her individual actions. Either she writes a letter to Santa Claus as if she is 100% convinced he exists, or she does not. She sits in his lap and makes her requests, or she refuses. She may leave for him milk and cookies or decline to do so; she cannot do both. Because her belief in Santa Claus affects her on a practical as well as an intellectual level, she is forced to make a choice between the two at every step she takes. It is impossible for her in any activity to remain on the fence. To do so would amount to no action at all. She may, because she is confused, act one day as if Santa Claus is coming and one day as if he is not, and we may all smile and write this off as part of a learning process that will end at the truth. None of us, however, will think it funny if she acts the same way twenty years later. We would all expect her by then to decide which is true and to act, even if she has some lingering doubts, as if she's right.

Belief in the existence of God is similar to the second example. It is not like the girl's belief in a moon of cheese, a purely intellectual concept which allows us to remain on the fence, forever holding its opposing views indecisively in our minds. It is much like the girl's belief in Santa Claus, an intellectual concept with practical implications. Every day we must decide whether to live as if God exists or as if He does not. No matter if we are 20% shy of certainty, we are forced each day in our individual actions to declare ourselves solidly in one camp or the other. Practically speaking, it is impossible to do otherwise. Like the girl in the example, we may initially be inconsistent, acting at times as if God is and later as if He is not. Like her, however, we would be expected within a reasonable time to practice one or the other exclusively, even if our percentage of certainty remained unchanged.

For anyone to remain an agnostic for long would be the height of impracticality. Eventually, a decision must be made one way or the other. Then and only then can a life of meaningful activity begin.

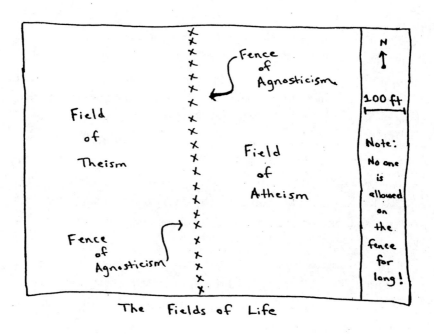

The Fields of Life

Figure 11:

The Impracticality of Agnosticism

Day 11
the impracticality of agnosticism (III)

"If God does not exist, then life is futile. If the God
of the Bible does exist, then life is meaningful...
Therefore, it seems to me that even if the evidence
for these two options were absolutely equal, a
rational person ought to choose Biblical Christianity."

- philosopher/theologian WILLIAM LANE CRAIG

Given the impracticality of agnosticism, it would seem the prudent course to remain a professing agnostic for as little time as possible. Admittedly, it is not uncommon in one's religious quest to spend some time as an agnostic while sorting out the evidence for and against God's existence. After such a sorting has been made, however, it does not behoove the seeker to tarry there any longer. The time has now arrived to stop balancing on the fence railing and to leap to one side of the pasture. The time has come to begin to exist as either a theist or an atheist.

A leap is the correct analogy here, for we have already asserted that the agnostic's search will end short of certainty, forcing him to choose theism or atheism based on the best evidence at hand. He may be only 80% convinced about one over the other, but that is plenty enough certainty upon which to make his choice. And to choose one or the other the agnostic *must* do, for to remain on the fence railing forever is lunacy. For one thing, nothing ever gets accomplished while straddling the fence. The work is done and the harvest gathered in the field. Secondly, it is impossible to stay on the fence 100% of the time. From time to time, all "fence- straddlers" lose their balance and fall to the ground, sometimes into one field and sometimes into the other. They appear quite pitiful to workers on either side of the fence as they go through their cycles: falling to one side, then climbing back on the railing, then falling again to one side or the other. At one moment they would seem to be theists but later, when they plunge to the other side, atheists. Their existence would serve no practical purpose whatsoever.

The agnostic, therefore, must make a decision and move away from the fence into one of the two fields. Only there can he or she have a meaningful existence. Only there will his or her life begin to make sense at all. Only at work in one of the fields will he or she complete the first leg of any religious quest, for only there can a final decision about God's existence be made. Even there he or she will be allowed to gaze occasionally at the workers on the other side and, if the work yonder begins to seem more attractive, to proceed to that field to work a while. You can rest assured, however, that in due time one side or the other will become his or her permanent home. That is how real life works, isn't it? We make choices, act upon them, reevaluate them, and finalize them through trial and error in the "fields" of life. Nothing is accomplished if nothing is chosen.[1]

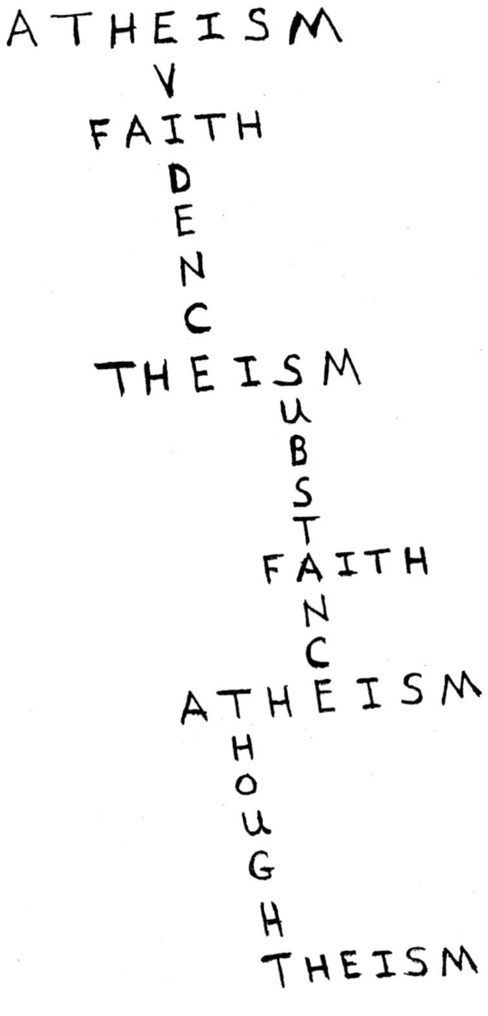

```
ATHEISM
   V
   FAITH
   D
   E
   N
   C
   THEISM
        u
        B
        S
        T
        FAITH
        N
        C
   ATHEISM
    H
    O
    u
    G
    H
      THEISM
```

Figure 12:

Evidence That Demands a Verdict

Day 12
an objective foundation

"Belief in God is genuinely coherent with all we know about ourselves and our universe."

- philosopher C. STEPHEN EVANS

There is a common misconception about faith in God that needs to be dispelled now and forever. Many people believe that anyone who puts his or her faith in God does so entirely from a subjective standpoint. They think that theists have no objective reasons to believe in God, that such belief has no rational component. They claim that there are no intellectual proofs whatsoever to support the existence of God. They are wrong.

Now there are many reasons to believe in God, and several of these reasons so happen to be purely subjective. The person may say, "I believe there is a God because something inside me says He exists." Or he or she may say, "I believe because it just feels right." This is subjective belief, and such subjectivity is usually present in all theists, including me. But this is not the whole story. In addition to my subjective reasons to believe in God, objective arguments exist. Rational reasons, intellectual "proofs," and concrete evidences are at hand to assist me and any other individual toward faith in God. This objective component must be acknowledged as well. In fact, in most cases it will serve as the supporting foundation upon which subjectivity will rest. Subjectivity alone carries little weight. Resting on a firm objective foundation, it can be very compelling.

The Bible (in the New Testament book of Hebrews) defines faith as "the *substance* of things hoped for, the *evidence* of things not seen." The *substance* and the *evidence* alluded to are objective, not subjective. Faith, then, is not mindless any more than it is emotionless. It includes both intellect and feelings, *evidence* as well as hearsay. As I convey to you in the following pages my reasons for believing in God, you will encounter both. I will give you objective reasons why I believe, rational arguments that compel me to believe. These are not my original arguments but are the classic "proofs of God" handed down to us over several hundred years by thinking men and women. I will not come up with new arguments but will try to present these old ones so that they can be understood by all. In addition, I will include in my arguments for God's existence some subjective reasons. These, I predict, will be very encouraging to any reader who is a theist and disquieting to anyone who is an atheist. They will be so, however, only after the objective reasons for God are explored. The foundation of the building must be laid first.

the **Argument from Design**

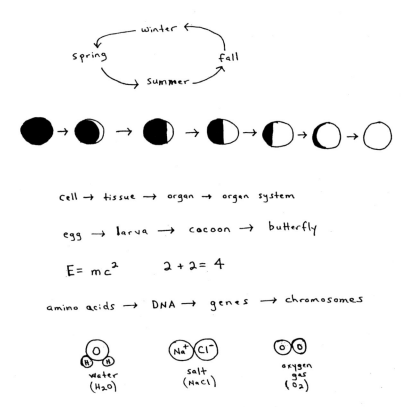

Figure 13:

The Design of the Universe

Day 13
the design of the universe

*"In a quiet revolution in thought and argument that
hardly anyone could have foreseen only two decades ago,
God is making a comeback... Now it is more respectable
among philosophers than it has been for a generation to
talk about the possibility of God's existence."*

- *Time* magazine ("Modernizing the Case for God")

We don't have to travel very far to begin our argument for God's
existence. All it takes is a nature walk. Come with me outdoors
and observe the natural world. Let us start early in the morning
when the dew is on the ground and end at midnight when the stars
are in the sky. During this excursion, we encounter evidence of
organization all around us. We see magnificent trees, appropriate
for the season of the year. We watch birds, ants, squirrels, and other
members of the animal world go about their daily activities. In
the light of day, we bask in the sun's glow and observe her steady
westward course through the sky. At nightfall, we gaze at the stars
in their galaxies and the moon in its predictable phase. When we
return from our walk, we are tired and fall quickly to sleep, our
intricate involuntary nervous systems keeping us alive without our
input. Upon arising the next day, we look in the mirror a little
more fascinated than the day before with ourselves and the natural
world around us.

Having made such a journey together, can we agree that the
universe in which we live gives evidence of organization and
design? Do you perceive with me order in the world and find it
easy to do so? Doesn't it seem the height of folly to look at nature
and deny such organization, order, and design? If you still have
any doubts (which is unlikely, for I have found almost universal
agreement on this point), take the time to spend thirty seconds
each thinking about the following: a rose, gravity, the human heart,

autumn, tides, comets, childbirth, the eye, a diamond, breathing, sleep, a butterfly, the atom, the harvest. After these seven minutes of contemplation, you will be convinced beyond a doubt that there is order, structure, and design in the world.

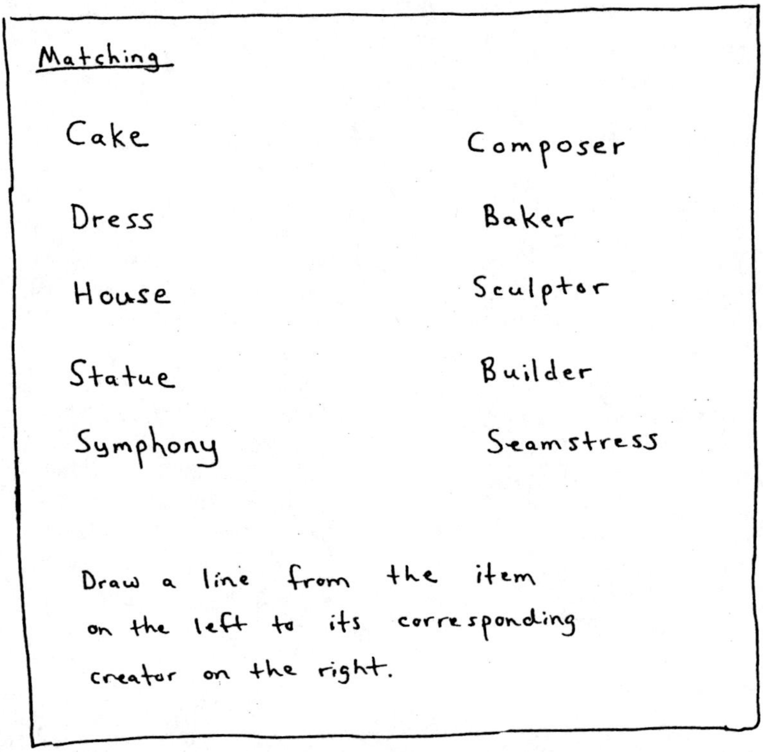

<u>Matching</u>

Cake   Composer

Dress   Baker

House   Sculptor

Statue   Builder

Symphony   Seamstress

Draw a line from the item
on the left to its corresponding
creator on the right.

Figure 14:
The Design-Designer Relationship

Day 14
the design-designer relationship

"I never asserted so absurd a proposition as that anything might arise without a cause."

- skeptic philosopher DAVID HUME

Now take a stroll with me down the streets of a small town. In doing so, we have traded the glory of nature, seen yesterday, for the marvels of commerce. As we proceed down Main Street, we pause briefly at its various businesses and window-shop. In several of the stores we make purchases and by the end of the day carry home with us the following items: a pocket watch, a dollhouse, a bicycle, a radio, and some fudge-nut brownies. We place these items on display inside our home and quickly notice that they have two things in common. First of all, they have order and design. Secondly, all of them appear to have been built, made, or fashioned by someone. You and I may not have seen these individuals in the town today, but this in no way makes us doubt that they exist. We know that somewhere there is a watchmaker, a dollhouse constructor, a bicycle manufacturer, a radio builder, and a sweet-toothed baker. It is intuitively obvious to us that these people *must* exist. We would, in fact, argue with anyone who entered our house and told us that they didn't. The presence of order and design in these purchased items screams to us that there has to be a "maker" and designer behind each.

This commonsense principle can be stated thusly: *evidence of design implies/demands the existence of a designer.* It is a principle that I find easy to grasp. It has the ring of truth to it. We must keep it in mind tomorrow when we take our third trip together, this time a sunset walk along a beach.

Figure 15:
The Argument from Design

Day 15
the classic argument

*"The mathematical precision of the universe
reveals the mathematical mind of God."*

- physicist ALBERT EINSTEIN

Imagine that you and I are walking at sunset along a lonely and deserted beach when you happen to come upon a watch half-buried in the sand. With curiosity you pick up the watch and examine it, noting it to be quite intricate. You discover that it is composed of various metals–silver, gold, and alloys–and of glass and crystal, all precisely molded or cut to a perfect fit. Glaring through the transparent face, you observe the fine movements of its small hands, each circling the numbered dial at its own monotonous pace. Not content to stop there, you open the watch to expose its innermost parts and therein discover an even more complex arrangement of small springs, spokes, and wheels, all aligned so as to propel the hands along their designated routes. You marvel at its beauty and complexity and begin to praise aloud the talents of the person who fashioned it. Hearing you, I angrily take the watch from you and tell you that it had no maker, that out of the earth's core spontaneously came forth metal and glass, that these materials somehow fashioned themselves into various shapes and sizes and then mysteriously set themselves into motions precise enough to reveal the time of day. I say all of this to you, and you call me a fool! You say that I have lost all touch with my reason and common sense, for *the very existence of such a watch implies the existence of a watchmaker.*

Now suppose that I put the watch aside, gaze toward the just-dark horizon, and show to you an even greater mechanism, a universe whose parts are planets, moons, and stars, all arranged with such precision that by their very movements tides are made to rise and fall, seasons to come and go, and day and night to alternate in predictable fashion. I show you this intricate mechanism and then hear you reply that there is no God, and I call *you* a fool! I say to you that your position is illogical, that it violates my sense of reason, that *the very existence of such a universe implies the existence of a Creator.*[1]

Figure 16:
Paley's Classic Defense of God

Day 16
the author's favorite

> *"I shall always be convinced that a watch proves a watch-maker, and that a universe proves a God."*

> - philosopher VOLTAIRE

A watch has organization and design; therefore, there must exist an organizer and designer (a watchmaker). The universe/natural world has organization and design; therefore, there must exist an Organizer and Designer (a Creator God). This is the classic *Argument from Design*. It was first introduced over two hundred years ago and has worn the test of time.[1] I am aware that atheists have attempted to pick it apart and discredit it (tomorrow, we will look at one of their rebuttals), but I have found nothing they say that compels me to abandon the argument as originally put forth. Unlike many theological arguments, it can be easily understood by all of us, both learned and unlearned, and bears the seal-of-approval of our common sense. It continues to be, after years of contemplation, my favorite argument for God's existence, the one I instinctively turn to first, the toughest one for the atheist to counter.

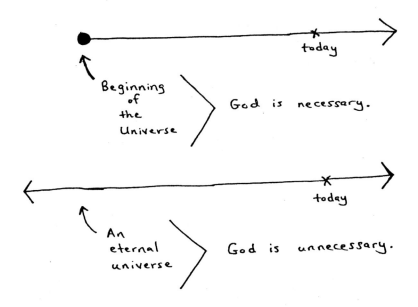

Figure 17:
One Answer of Atheists
to the Argument from Design

Day 17
the atheist's 1ˢᵗ rebuttal: an eternal universe

*"There may be some theoretical chance that wind
and rain erosion could produce the faces of the four
presidents on the side of a mountain, but it is still far
more probable to assume that an intelligent sculptor
created Mount Rushmore."*

- philosopher NORMAN GEISLER

One answer of the atheist to the *Argument from Design* has been the assertion that the universe itself had no beginning, that it "always was and always will be" and thus would require no God to create or sustain it. The analogy here is of a watch with no beginning, eternally in motion, needing no assistance from any outside source to bring it into being or keep it running. The universe, says the atheist, could possibly be such an eternal, self-perpetuating entity, negating the need for God. There could be evidence of design and organization in its component parts (for example, a rainbow or a snowflake) because the basic nature of the universe is that of design. Stated another way, the universe as a whole is, always has been, and always will be an organized universe. The small evidences of organization we see within it every day are merely fragments of the whole. Thus, when I argue that evidence of design in the universe proves the existence of a Designer, the atheist is not phased. The existence of design in the universe, the atheist counters, could merely imply the existence of an eternal universe of design.

Every time I hear this rebuttal, it appears to me somewhat circular in its logic. Still, it is plausible that the universe, if it is eternal and self-sustaining, could enact on its own the uniform laws of nature, could plot on its own the precise course of the celestial bodies, and could be responsible on its own for the magnificence of the human body. It certainly is possible, if indeed the universe is eternal and self-sustaining.

But, though plausible, is it likely? Think with me again of the watch, bicycle, dollhouse, radio, and fudge brownies alluded to earlier. We could try to get out of admitting the existence of a maker for these items if we assumed that they were a piece or fragment of a larger eternal item of the same character. We could assume that our watch was merely a part of the Eternal Watch, that the bicycle came from the Great Bicycle, that the radio was a subset of the Grand Radio, that the dollhouse was a fragment of the Universal Mansion, and that the brownie was a square off the Infinite Planar Cookie Sheet. We could assume, even propagate, these theories because they are possible, but can we really take them seriously? Do they make sense to us? Do they have the ring of truth to them? No, they do not. Something is not to be considered likely just because that something is possible.

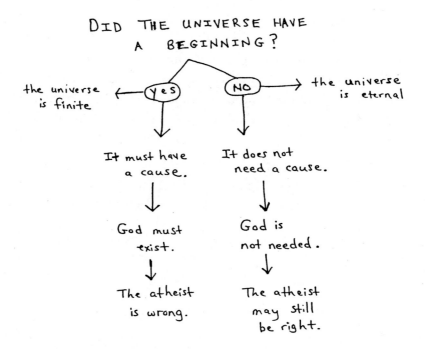

Figure 18:

A Finite Universe – the Atheist's Nightmare

Day 18
the atheist's nightmare: a finite universe

"...the universe itself is the ultimate explainer."

- atheist ANTONY G. N. FLEW

This is one of three routes atheists use to discredit the *Argument from Design*. (We will look at the other two shortly.) They claim, and rightly so, that the *Argument from Design* would not apply to a universe that is eternal and self-sustaining. There would be no need for God the Creator if the universe was never created, no need for God the Designer if the nature of that eternal universe is one of design, no need for God the Sustainer if the universe is self-sustaining. On this "ultimate" universe, as Flew above describes it, all atheists pin their hopes.

Conversely, a universe with a definite beginning places atheists in a real dilemma. They know all too well that a finite universe begs the existence of God, for such a universe as ours could not arise on its own and keep itself running. If the universe is not eternal, they would suddenly find themselves in irrational quicksand with only two options of rescue available to them:

1. they could embrace the *Argument from Design* and begin to believe in God, or
2. they could continue to deny Him while searching elsewhere for ways to discredit the theist.

In other words, they could reconsider or retreat.

Figure 19:
Celebrating the Birth of the Universe

Day 19
the answer of science

*"...the older idea of an eternally existing world
is now known to have a problem. These
measurements of what scientists call the
background radiation that fills the universe
tell us that the world is not eternal, but that
it actually had a beginning."*

- research scientist ROBERT GANGE

A finite universe, one with a definite beginning, is a nightmare for the atheist. He or she can ignore the *Argument from Design* if the universe is chronologically infinite. An eternal universe would need no Creator, just as an eternal watch would need no watchmaker. If the universe and watch are finite, however, then there must have been a Creator and a watchmaker. A universe with a beginning brings the atheist face-to-face with an irrefutable *Argument from Design* and thus face-to-face with God. At that point, to continue to deny God's existence could only be attributed to obstinacy, stupidity, or insanity. Only stubborn, ignorant, or delusional individuals act against reason.

Ironically, the problem here for the atheist is science itself, for the current trend–based on the evidence at hand and espoused by the leaders of the scientific world–is to assume that the universe did have a beginning. From the Big Bang Theory to other lesser-known hypotheses, the physicists present to us a universe that most likely is *not* eternal, one that had a definite birth billions of years ago.[1]

This places the atheist in an obvious predicament. An eternal universe is what he needs to refute the *Argument from Design*. Science, usually the atheist's megaphone, proclaims a universe with a beginning. To remain an atheist in the face of such current evidence, he is forced to disagree with all the talk about a finite universe–and be accused of turning his back on science–or to agree with the scientists that the universe had a beginning–and (in light of the *Argument from Design*) be accused of turning away from his own common sense.

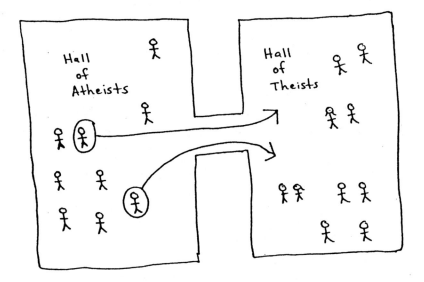

Figure 20:
Changing Rooms

Day 20
from atheist to theist

> *"Today, it seems to me, there is no good reason for*
> *an intelligent person to embrace the illusion of*
> *atheism or agnosticism, to make the same*
> *intellectual mistakes I made. I wish...I had*
> *known then what I know now."*

- scientist and former atheist PATRICK GLYNN

If the universe needs to be eternal to make atheism plausible and if the scientific evidence declares that it is not, then one would expect to find honest men and women of learning who once were atheists but have changed their position in light of the evidence before them. We would expect to find men and women who are intelligent enough to see that atheism is not logical or rational in a finite universe, men and women who are brave enough to admit they were wrong about God and change their tune. We would expect to find such people, if what I have said is true, and we do.

Take, for example, Patrick Glynn. He is Harvard-educated and the Associate Director and Scholar-in-Residence at the George Washington University Institute for Communitarian Policy Studies. He is a former atheist who, because of the scientific evidence before him, has become a Christian. In fact, he wrote a book, entitled *God: The Evidence*, in which he says, "Today, the concrete data point strongly in the direction of the God hypothesis...Those who oppose it have no testable theory to marshal... Ironically, the picture of the universe bequeathed to us by the most advanced twentieth-century science is closer in spirit to the vision presented in the Book of Genesis than anything offered by science since Copernicus."

Along with Glynn, you can now include Antony Flew as one of the most recent converts to theism. For over fifty years this British philosopher has argued against the existence of God. He has written volume after volume and participated in debate after debate giving evidence that God is not real. Aware of his reputation as "the atheist's atheist," I included one of his quotes as a preface to Day 18's reading. At the time I did so, I had no idea that Flew, now 81, was in the process of changing his mind about God. Exactly one week before I sent this book to be published, my father handed me an article that spotlighted this renowned atheist's 180-degree theological turn. Flew made his startling announcement in a fall term 2004 group discussion at New York University. "[I]t seems to me," he boldly declared, "that the case for [a] God who has the characteristics of power and also intelligence is now much stronger than it ever was before." Unable to maintain his atheism in the light of recent scientific evidence in favor of God, Flew's newly embraced theism is, according to theology and philosophy professor Gary Habermas, "testimony to the many, especially scientific figures, who are coming [to God] by way of intelligent design…The fact that he has become a theist is testimony to the type of evidence we have for God's existence today."

I could relate to you numerous other examples of ex-atheists, men and women of learning who have made the switch to theism because it made the most sense to them scientifically and philosophically. The point I am trying to make is that such men and women do exist and that this is what you would expect to see if atheism proposes an eternal universe and science proposes the opposite. I am not blind to the fact that there have been other men and women who have made the switch in the opposite direction, from theism to atheism, and have done so because the latter makes the most sense to them. I realize that the atheist could quote them as readily as I have quoted Patrick Glynn and Antony Flew above. Their change from atheism to belief in God does not in any way prove that God exists. It does, however, drive home the fact that belief in God is possible from a scientific, evidential standpoint, not just an emotional, subjective one. That, I think, is a huge step in the right direction. Far too long has the assumption been made that science and reason are exclusively the tools of the atheist.

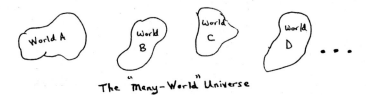

The "Many-World" Universe

The "Accordion" Universe

Figure 21:

Alternate Theories of the Universe

Day 21
alternate theories of the universe

"...the fine-tuning of the universe points powerfully toward an Intelligent Designer–and some people will hypothesize anything to avoid reaching that conclusion."

- philosopher/theologian WILLIAM LANE CRAIG

The *Argument from Design* presents a tough challenge to atheists. They know that the presence of design in a watch mandates the existence of a watchmaker. They must admit that there is evidence of design in the universe. How, then, can they say that this universe of design had no Maker?

We have already seen two ways that atheists have addressed this dilemma. The first is to theorize an eternal universe, one with no beginning, a universe that always was and thus would require no Maker to bring it into being. The problem with this, we have noted, is recent scientific evidence that the universe is *not* eternal, that it had a definite beginning in time. The second way atheists have addressed this inconsistency is to admit that they were wrong about the universe and to conclude, based on the logic of the *Argument from Design,* that there must be a God behind it. We have observed that a number of atheists for this very reason have converted to theism, and we have given quotes from two such individuals.

The majority of atheists, however, still refuse to believe in God. Steadfast and determined, they have looked at the evidence pointing toward a finite universe and tried to find ways to refute it. In so doing, they have come up with some alternate theories that reveal how the universe can *appear* to be finite yet really be eternal.

One of their theories is commonly called the *Many Worlds Hypothesis.*[1] It states that our universe may be just one of a legion of universes, and while ours may indeed have had a definite beginning, the conglomerate of universes did not. The proponents of this hypothesis claim that the universe as we know it arose from the conglomerate, much like a drop of water arises from the sea. When our universe ends, it will be reabsorbed into the eternal whole.

A second alternate theory is what I call the *Accordion Universe Hypothesis*, usually referred to as the Oscillating Model.[2] The universe, this theory claims, is very much like an eternal accordion in motion, sometimes expanding and sometimes contracting but always existing. Its nature is one of eternal oscillation. Going through cycles of compression, then expansion–each cycle lasting billions of years–our universe could very well be eternal but appear to be finite. What science sees today as its definite beginning would simply be one of the points where it is maximally compressed and begins to change direction.

I am not about to attempt to weigh the merits of these alternative theories. That is the job of the scientists. What I do want to do is to make you realize something that is as obvious as the nose on your face: the fact that atheists have had to come up with these theories to explain the eternal nature of the universe is testimony enough that the *Argument from Design* is a formidable challenge to them. In fact, if it were ever proven that the universe had a beginning, the atheist would have no intellectual recourse but to throw up his or her hands in surrender to the theist. If spiritually receptive, he or she would have no reasonable response than to join the theist, genuflected in reverence before the reality of God.

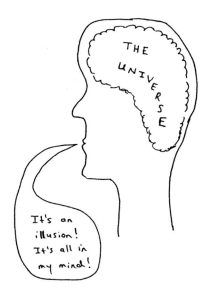

Figure 22:
Another Answer of Atheists to the Argument from Design

Day 22
the atheist's 2nd rebuttal: an illusory universe

*"...a student at New York University...troubled his
professor with a contradictory question, 'Sir, how do
you know that I exist?' The professor paused for a while,
lowered his glasses, gazed at the student and demanded,
'And whom shall I say is asking?'"*

- apologist STEVE KUMAR

There is yet another way the atheist may try to rebut the *Argument
from Design.* Instead of proposing new hypotheses that leave open
the possibility of an eternal universe, he or she may claim that the
universe doesn't exist at all. The whole universe, it may be argued,
could just be an illusion, and there would be no need for God if
this were so. Only things that exist need a creator.

If you think that this is somewhat fanciful and far-fetched and
that no thinking person could find it believable, then look at the
Eastern religion of Buddhism. Many of its millions of adherents
have tried to deal with the reality of evil in the world by rejecting
its existence, saying that it is but an illusion. If people can believe
that all the pain and suffering in the world, even their own, is not
real, would it be a huge leap to proclaim the whole universe to be
illusory? No, it would not.

The problems with this line of thinking are twofold. First of
all, no one lives his or her life consistent with this hypothesis.
As Norman Geisler explains, "They may maintain that all is an
illusion, but if one were to push them in front of an oncoming bus,
they would quickly 'warm up' to the reality idea!" "Accepting the
illusionist's position," he says, "demands that one admit that all of
life as he experiences it is deceiving him."

In addition to the problems it poses from a practical standpoint,
the *illusion theory* doesn't make sense philosophically. If you believe
the entire universe to be an illusion, then you must also believe

that your mind, a part of that universe, is not real. How, then, could you ever perceive the universe to be so? Is it consistent for you to say at one moment that your mind and all the thoughts it produces are illusions and then claim a moment later that this one thought– "the world is but an illusion"–*is* real? "All the world is an illusion" cannot be held to be true. If it were true, no one could possibly know it. This obvious flaw was the source of René Descartes' famous assertion: "I think; therefore, I am." He knew all too well that his own thoughts made an illusory world impossible.

I am not in any way implying that the majority of atheists have embraced the view that the universe doesn't exist. In fact, not many have. During the Enlightenment, both theists (like Descartes) and skeptics (like David Hume) dismissed this illusory hypothesis as impractical and nonsensical. What I am relating to you is how a few atheists, hoping to find some way to negate the need for a Creator of the universe, have resorted to the silly notion that the universe is no universe at all. It is amazing the lengths some people will go before admitting they are wrong.

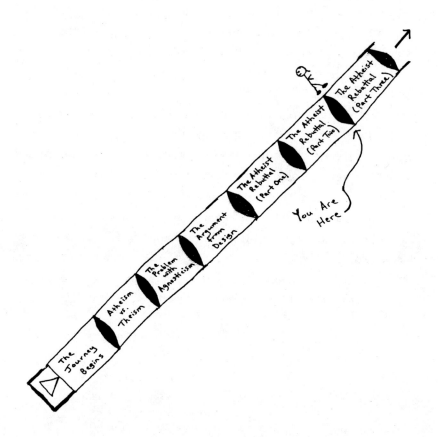

Figure 23:
A Look Back

Day 23
a review of Days 1-22

"The heavens declare the glory of God; the skies proclaim the work of His hands. Day after day they pour forth speech; night after night they display knowledge."

- the PSALMIST

I said at the very start (Day 1) that the first phase of anyone's religious search must be the question of God's existence. I think now would be a good time to pause and review just how far we've come on our journey. We have presented theism and atheism as the only two possible destinations, describing the latter as "anti-religion," a system of beliefs with no spiritual core (Day 2). We have considered the advantages of theism over atheism, the principal two being that only in the former can anyone hope for life after death or eventual justice for all (Days 3-5). We have declared such hope futile, however, if it turns out the atheist is right and the theist wrong (Day 6). We have discussed the limitations of all arguments for and against God, admitting that neither the atheist nor the theist can disprove or prove God's existence beyond a shadow of a doubt (Days 7-8). In so doing, we have raised the possibility that agnosticism could be the only honest recourse and have come to the conclusion that it is intellectually acceptable but pragmatically impossible to forever waffle about God's existence, that, in the final analysis, agnosticism should only serve as a step toward theism or atheism (Day 9). We have informed agnostics that the only reasonable and practical thing to do is to declare a position and begin to live as if that position were true, always possessing the option to defect to the other camp if it is necessary to do so to make their final choice (Days 10-11). A permanent choice, we have said, is one that can only be made while "working in the fields," not while straddling the fence, and it is a choice that everyone expects them to make in due time.

In an effort to help you make that choice between theism and atheism, we have dispelled the myth that it is purely a subjective decision and have proposed that rational arguments, scientific evidence, and commonsense axioms exist that can form the foundation of our beliefs (Day 12). We have taken three excursions together, two into nature and another into town, and have come to the conclusion that the presence of design in an object (whether that object is natural or commercial) demands the presence of a designer (Days 13-14) and that, given our universe's obvious design, an Intelligent Designer–God the Creator–must be behind it (Day 15-16). We have seen that this *Argument from Design* poses a significant problem to the atheist, who must assert, in spite of scientific evidence to the contrary, that the universe is eternal and in need of no Creator to bring it into existence (Days 17-18, 21); or must admit that it is indeed finite and become a theist, as several atheists have done (Day 20); or must come up with the self-refuting notion that the universe needs no Creator because it is nonexistent, a mere illusion (Day 22).

That is how far we have come on our journey, but we have just started this first leg of our religious quest. We must cover much more ground in the next few days. In addition to the *Argument from Design,* we will look at four other arguments for God's existence and examine the atheist's response to them. Before we do so, however, we need to address the most common retort given by atheists when confronted with the *Argument from Design.*

Figure 24:

A Third Answer of the Atheist to the Argument from Design

Day 24
the atheist's 3rd rebuttal: a disordered
universe

> *"Not many years ago, when I was an atheist, if anyone
> had asked me, 'Why do you not believe in God?' my
> reply would run something like this: 'Look at the
> universe we live in… If you ask me to believe that
> this is the work of a benevolent and omnipotent
> spirit, I reply that all the evidence points in the
> opposite direction.'"*

> - Christian C. S. LEWIS in *The Problem of Pain*

The universe, in addition to its intricate design, also bears the marks of disorder and disarray. This is the most common counter-argument used by the atheist to defuse the *Argument from Design*. Almost as an immediate reflex, he or she will point toward the same heavens we used earlier to prove the universe's design and remind us that from these same skies come tornadoes, hurricanes, and other natural calamities that turn its very design into chaos. When we point to the intricate human machine, he or she will take us to the oncology unit of the hospital and show us human machines gone very bad. When we say that the presence of design in the universe demands the presence of God, he or she will reply that the presence of such chaos in the universe declares just as much that He is not present.

Each of us easily recognizes that this is a formidable objection to the *Argument from Design*. As a resident of Alabama, I vividly recall a day several years ago when—on a Palm Sunday morning in a rural Methodist church in the small town of Piedmont—a tornado destroyed the building and took the lives of several little children, all sitting in the front pews awaiting their turn to participate in the service. One of the deceased was the daughter of the minister there. If there is a God who is an Intelligent Designer, how could this ever happen? Doesn't this very tragedy deny His existence? As an emergency physician, I have treated several individuals from my town who were injured by another tornado and have witnessed death at its hands. I have also seen the ravages of diseases which appear to inflict men, women, and children indiscriminately, and I can understand why anyone at their bedsides would wonder if God is there. We cannot ignore such events and their theological implications. We must meet them head-on. If not, we appear to have lost considerable ground on our journey.

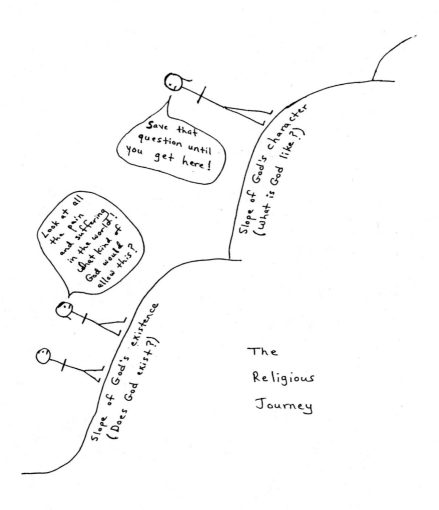

Figure 25:
Good Question, Wrong Time

Day 25
good question, wrong time (I)

"Since God is the one who directly creates everything, why does He create famines, earthquakes, mud slides, AIDS, deformed babies, and the like?"

- skeptic EDWARD BOYD, in a letter to his Christian son

I have an answer for any atheist who claims that evidence of disarray in the universe makes the *Argument from Design* meaningless. I acknowledge that such disorder exists and am not blind to the misery unleashed by it, nor do I flippantly dismiss it as unimportant. It is, in fact, of supreme importance to any religious seeker, for the theological problems it poses can shake even the strongest faith. Most assuredly, we *must* deal with its implications at some time during our pilgrimage.

This first leg of our journey, however, is not the time. We are presently ascending the slope of God's existence, and the plain truth is that the reality of suffering, as important as it is, has no bearing on that subject. It is irrelevant to our present discussion. Consequently, it does not weaken the *Argument from Design* one bit.

When analyzed in-depth, all this finger-pointing by atheists is readily exposed as an attempt to deceive and distract. Like everyone else, they must admit that there is design in the world. Failure to do so is analogous to the ostrich burying its head in the sand. Unless the universe is eternal or illusory, they must also admit that the presence of this design demands the existence of a Designer. Having made these admissions, they then proceed to divert attention away from the design and toward the just-as-obvious disarray. They say to us, "Look at this disorder! It makes the question of God's existence easy. He cannot be said to exist in the face of such discord."

What theists must realize is that when atheists argue thusly, they argue illogically. They raise a good question but do so at the wrong time. I believe that the fallacy of their argument is easy to grasp. Given the propensity of atheists to almost universally resort to this defense, its irrationality must be exposed before we can proceed full-speed ahead. A commonsense illustration will be used tomorrow to shed light on the truth.

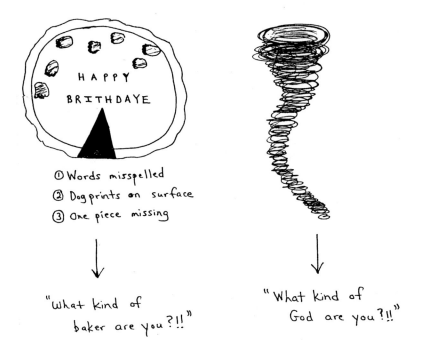

Figure 26:

The Correct Question When the Design Is Not Perfect

Day 26
good question, wrong time (II)

"A loving God could not possibly be the author of the horrors we have been describing... [I]t is obvious that there cannot be a loving God."

- atheist CHARLES TEMPLETON

Imagine that you enter a bakery and notice on one of its tables a three-tiered wedding cake. You marvel at its design, noting it to be one of the most beautiful cakes you have ever seen. Its three cylindrical sections, the largest on the bottom and the smallest at the top, are aligned with such precision that there is not even a hint of asymmetry. Upon them the snow-white icing is spread as smooth as the surface of a pond on a calm day. Bordering each section at its circumference is more icing, strands of pink in a rope-like configuration. You smile as you observe on top of the cake's surface the ornate bride and groom figurines, facing each other as if repeating their vows.

Now imagine that you look around and see that the bakery is devoid of life, save for a small dog lying beside the doorway. Would you, in the absence of anyone in the room, surmise that the wedding cake before you had no baker, that its ingredients threw themselves into three cake pans, baked themselves until done, arranged themselves vertically on the table, and then decorated themselves in so elaborate a fashion? Of course, not! Wouldn't you assume that somewhere a baker existed who was responsible for this cake? If you were to ask any question at this time, would it not be "Where is the baker?" instead of "Does the baker exist?"? The mere existence of a cake of such intricate design would prove to you the existence of a baker. This, applied to the universe, is the *Argument from Design.*

Needing a cake the next week for your son's birthday, imagine further that you leave a note on the table asking the baker to fashion one as elaborate as the wedding cake you happened to see. When you return the day before the birthday, you enter through the same doorway past the same dog and see on the same table a birthday cake you assume to be yours. It, too, is a three-tiered cake with white icing and colored trim, this time blue. It is adorned with seven candles at the top with the words "Happy Birthday" engraved around them.

You at first seem very pleased with the cake until you step closer to the table and notice the paw prints on its surface. You quickly surmise that after the cake was placed on the table, the dog (perhaps while chasing a cat) must have leaped upon it and raced across it, in the process destroying its perfection. Because of this canine romp, your birthday cake appears to be in some disorder and disarray. Understandably, you would become angry and disturbed and (although no one is present in the bakery to hear you) would begin to air your objections aloud.

Consider the kind of remarks you would make. Would you, in light of the evidence before you, begin to scream at the top of your lungs, "There is no baker! The baker doesn't exist!"? No, you would not. The disarray of the cake would not cause you to doubt the baker's existence whatsoever. Your remarks would instead be more like this: "What kind of baker would leave a cake unprotected on this table? What kind of baker would let a dog (and perhaps a cat) ransack his creation? What kind of baker would allow this to happen?" While the disorder evident on the cake's surface would not cause you to question the baker's existence, it would cause you to call into question the baker's character.

In the same way, the obvious evidence of disorder in the universe does not in the least call into question God's existence. Atheists cannot look at the admixture of design and disarray before them and scream, "There is no God! God doesn't exist!," any more that you could doubt the baker's existence based on the imperfect cake. In light of such imperfection, the character of God, rather than His existence, is called into question. "What kind of God would allow disorder into His universe? Does He not have the power to prevent it from happening, or does He just not care?" These are the type of questions raised by suffering.

Thus, when the atheist points toward an imperfect universe and denies God's existence, he is running ahead of the group. He is asking a good question ("What is God's nature?") at the wrong time (on the first leg of our journey when the only question before us is: "Does God exist?"). In effect, he is diverting our attention from the subject at hand. We should encourage him to return to the group and concentrate on the present. He must save his question for a later date.

Evidence of disorder in the universe, it turns out, does not hinder the reality of God. The *Argument from Design* still stands.

1. Is there a God?

2. What kind of God is He?

Figure 27:

First Things First!

Day 27
good question, wrong time (III)

"This world doesn't look at all like the kind of world we'd have if there were an all-powerful, all-loving God behind it."

- EDWARD K. BOYD in *Letters from a Skeptic*

"No one who has nursed cancer patients can believe in God."

- quote from a NURSE in *Why Do Men Suffer?*

"My argument against God was that the universe seemed so cruel and unjust."

- former atheist C. S. LEWIS

"Is it possible to believe that there is a loving or caring Creator when all this woman needed was rain?*"*

- atheist CHARLES TEMPLETON, looking at a *Life* magazine photograph of a drought-stricken African woman holding her dead child

When I say that the universe's disarray has no bearing on the existence of God, I am not trying to minimize the reality of suffering and pain in the world. The presence of such widespread agony cannot be dismissed or ignored, for it is a reality that sooner or later we all will experience in full force. Philosopher Elton Trueblood describes it as "a problem which no theist can avoid and no honest thinker will try to avoid." I cannot, however, let sentiment about this subject rule over reason. It is obvious to me that the reality of pain and suffering in this world does not bring God's existence into question any more than the presence of that faulty cake in yesterday's illustration brought into question the existence of the baker. It is the character of God, not His reality, that is put on trial by suffering. People tend to look at all the pain and suffering in the world and ask, "Is there really a God?," when the appropriate question to raise, the only rational question, is: "What kind of God are You?"

When we get around to discussing the nature of God, we must address the presence in the universe of disorder and disarray, of pain and suffering, of disease, war, and calamity. But that is not our present destination. It will have to come later. We have not yet fully ascended the slope of God's existence. While the four quotations preceding today's reading may be unsettling to us, we must recognize them for what they are (questions about God's character) and not let them distract us from the issue at hand. As the old adage urges, "First things first."

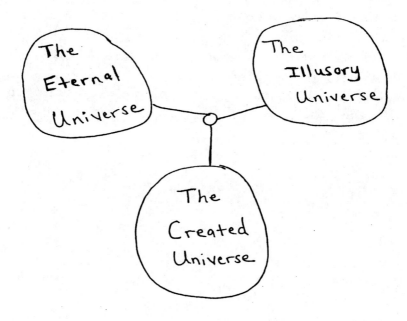

Figure 28:
The Three Alternatives

Day 28
the universe: three alternatives

"The fact of evil in no way eliminates the reality of God."

- apologist STEVE KUMAR

It turns out, then, that all the commotion made by atheists about the disorder in the universe is nothing but an attempt at diversion. All they are attempting to do is to get us off-track, to distract us from the subject at hand. That subject is whether or not God exists. Regarding it, we have already concluded that the universe's intricate design, acknowledged by theists and atheists alike, implies the presence of a Designer God. This implication does not change if His universe appears to have some design flaws. It is God's character, a later subject, that is called into question by these "flaws," not His existence. Any design-gone-bad is still a design and must have a designer behind it.

When faced with the *Argument from Design,* the atheist is thus left with only three rational alternatives:

1. He or she may claim that the universe is eternal and in no need of a Designer;
2. He or she may claim that the universe is an illusion and in no need of a Designer;
3. He or she may admit that the universe had a beginning and requires a Designer.

These are the only options open to the atheist. As far as I am concerned, he or she does not have the option of turning our attention to the universe's disarray. That is merely a diversionary tactic. From a rational standpoint, that disarray has everything to do with God's nature, but it has no bearing at all on His existence. The sooner the religious seeker sees this, the better.

the Argument from Fairness

Figure 29:

The Universal Cry of Humanity

Day 29
the argument defined

"Two things fill the mind with ever new and increasing admiration and awe...the starry heavens above me and the moral law within me."

- philosopher IMMANUEL KANT

The *Argument from Design* is just one rational defense of God's existence. In my opinion, it is the easiest to understand and the most difficult to rebut of such arguments and is the one I usually turn to first in a theological discussion. Other arguments do exist, and the time has come for us to look at them. I think you will likewise find them to be rational and comprehensible. Together with the *Argument from Design,* they present a formidable challenge to any atheist.

To introduce the next argument, pretend that you and I ask a friend of yours to join us for a game of Monopoly. During the course of the game, I roll a "seven" with the dice, but instead of moving my game piece seven spaces forward, I move it ahead a full nine squares. When you question my move, I respond, "I know I rolled a 'seven,' but I needed to land on Boardwalk, so I moved up nine spaces instead." The unison reply from you and your friend would be, "That's not fair!" Somehow the three of us manage to make amends and resume our board game, but I continue to violate the rules and act in ways both of you consider to be unjust. Finally, having had your fill of such antics, you and your friend tell me that the game is over and you are going home.

After you leave, I begin to think about my actions and recognize that I have behaved badly. I fear that I have jeopardized our friendship and, in sincere remorse, come to your house and beg forgiveness. As evidence of my sincerity, I offer to you and your friend a free dinner with me at a local restaurant. Your response is that you will not forgive me, even if I offered you the Hope diamond. Then you snatch the dinner coupons from my hand and tell me that you and your friend will enjoy dinner at my expense but that I am not welcome. After slamming the door shut in my face, I yell to you through it, "That's not fair!"

My argument will be: (1) that given the right set of circumstances, every person who has ever lived in history could be driven to say, "That's not fair!"; (2) that making an accusation of unfairness implies that fairness must also exist; (3) that when the atheist looks at the apparent injustice in the universe and screams, "That's not fair!," he or she is admitting that somewhere justice exists; and (4) that justice (which includes morality, the sense that some things are right and some things are wrong) cannot exist unless God exists.[1]

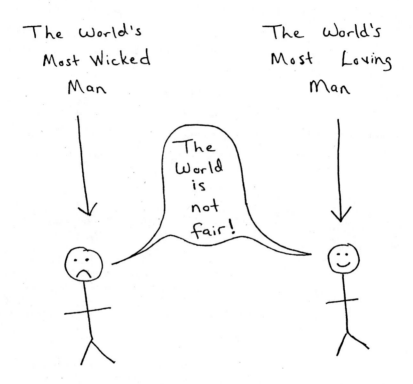

Figure 30:
No Exceptions!

Day 30
Point One: life is unfair

*"This is not fair! This is not just! I shouldn't be graded
on the color of the cover but on the content of the paper."*

- a philosophy student (after writing a research paper on
the absence of absolute right and wrong) to his teacher
(who gave him an "F" because he didn't like blue covers)

I believe it next to impossible to go through life without the
phrase "That's not fair!" crossing your lips. I know most of us need
only replay the past twenty-four hours to note the last time a sense
of unfairness entered our minds. My first point in what I call the
Argument from Fairness is that everyone has this innate sense that
some things are unfair. I believe it is universal, as sure as the sun
setting in the west.

Most of you will see rather quickly that this is true. There are
some of you, I presume, who may counter that some of history's
most evil men may have been so blind to justice that the thought of
fairness and unfairness never entered their minds. The reason they
acted so badly, you say, is that no such sense of justice was ever a
part of them. Think with me a little, and you will see that you are
wrong, that even the vilest people this earth has ever known have
looked around about them and cried, "That's not fair!"

Take, for example, Adolf Hitler. Although we can never in any
way condone the holocaust he inflicted, is it not easy to recognize
that he did so in part because his warped mind believed it unfair for
Jews to have political and economic advantage over the "superior"
Aryan race? When he looked at the world around him, he said, in
essence, "That's not fair!" Or take the terrorists who destroyed the
Twin Towers and the innocent lives of thousands in the process.
Did they not act because they sensed it was not fair for the United
States to have such a dominant place in the world? Didn't they also
cry, "That's not fair!"? What about the men who conspired to have

Jesus crucified? Did they not act on the premise that it was not fair for anyone to make the sort of claims he was making and get away with it? As they heard him speak, they thought, "That's not fair!"

Now I want to make sure that no one misunderstands me. In no shape, form, or fashion am I saying that any of these people were justified in their actions. I am not saying that they were right; in fact, I believe strongly that they were 100% wrong when they committed these infamous acts. Just because someone thinks he or she has been treated unfairly does not make it a fact. Furthermore, even if it were a fact, such unfairness does not give anyone license to retaliate with acts of injustice exponentially greater. What I am trying to show you, while acknowledging how vehemently opposed every fiber of my being is to the horrors these men inflicted, is that even they, some of the most evil men who ever lived, acted so because they felt life was unjust. They, like everyone else in the world, uttered the phrase, "That's not fair!"

The atheist is no exception. We have just finished discussing how he or she, in an attempt to counter the *Argument from Design,* almost always refers us to the sickness, natural calamity, and heinous evil in the world. We have concluded that such evidence of disarray in the universe has no rational bearing on God's existence (the subject of the *Argument from Design)* but has everything to do with His character. The atheist is asking God a good question–"What kind of God would let this happen?"–and, in so doing, is accusing Him of injustice. The atheist, too, says, "That's not fair!"

So it is with the whole of mankind.

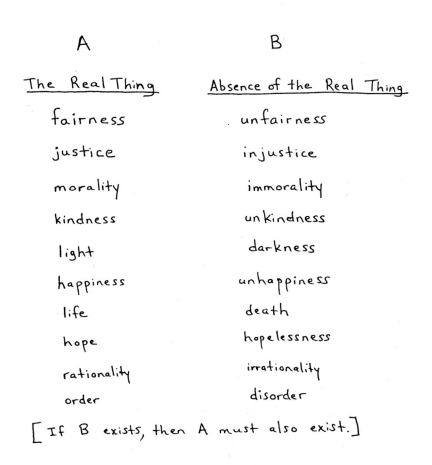

A	B
<u>The Real Thing</u>	<u>Absence of the Real Thing</u>
fairness	unfairness
justice	injustice
morality	immorality
kindness	unkindness
light	darkness
happiness	unhappiness
life	death
hope	hopelessness
rationality	irrationality
order	disorder

[If B exists, then A must also exist.]

Figure 31:

How Fairness and Unfairness Are Related

Day 31
Point Two: fairness exists

"The point we dare not miss about that story [of the philosophy student and his teacher] is that it pretty accurately depicts how every person claiming to believe that morality is subjective acts when an injustice is done to him or her."

- religious philosopher PAUL CHAMBERLAIN

Men and women have forever looked at the universe around them and thought, "That's not fair!" Even those people who claim that there is no absolute right and wrong in the world (and, therefore, no such thing as fairness and unfairness) act in their day-to-day lives as if there is. Take, for example, the philosophy student quoted yesterday. When push came to shove, he accused his teacher of unfairness. He could not apply the premise of his research paper to real life. This, of course, was the point the teacher was trying to make to him, the reason he gave him a failing grade for such a frivolous reason. And it is the first point I am trying to make to you. *Everyone knows intuitively that life is not fair, and everyone acts in a manner consistent with that intuition.*

The second point I want to make follows from the first, namely that *it is impossible for something to be unfair unless fairness also exists.* I think this is not hard to grasp and should not take up a lot of our time. How could you and your friend complain that I was being unfair in Monopoly unless you had some notion that fairness existed? How could I scream through the shut door, "That's not fair!" unless I believed that something else was? How could Hitler, the Islamic terrorists, and the angry mob at the cross consider themselves to be correcting injustices unless they believed that such a thing as justice existed, too? They could not, and neither can you. It is irrational to claim that there is no such thing as fairness in the universe and then say a minute later that something is unfair. That is what the philosophy student tried to do, and he appeared rather foolish in the process. As soon as he complained that the grade on his paper was unfair, he made it clear to the teacher that a better grade, an "A" or a "B", was fair. The whole premise of his thesis, that there exists no such thing in this world as right/wrong or fair/unfair, turned out to be a lie exposed by his very actions.

Unfairness cannot exist without fairness as its standard. You cannot have the first without the possibility of the second. To say that unfairness exists but fairness does not is like saying that bad exists but good does not, hate exists but love does not, dark exists but light does not, losing exists but winning does not, death exists but life does not. Such thinking is nonsensical. It's a waste of anyone's time.

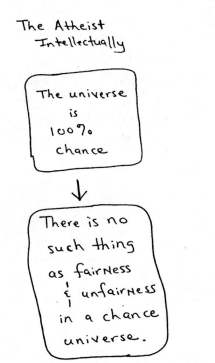

Figure 32:
The Atheist's Contradiction
Regarding Justice

Day 32
Point Three: 1 and 2 apply to the atheist

"The problem with [the statement that nothing is absolutely right or wrong] is...that it refutes itself. It is something like the statement 'I can't speak a word of English.' By speaking the sentence, I refute it."

- philosopher PAUL CHAMBERLAIN

Thus far we have laid down two of the four principles of the *Argument from Fairness,* my second defense of God's existence. We have observed that people have a universal sense that certain things are unfair, and we have noted that if such unfairness is a reality, fairness must also be real. Anyone who labels one thing in this universe "unfair" but then claims there is no sense of justice in the universe is being illogical. His or her statement is irrational. If unfairness exists, fairness must exist as well.

My third point takes these first two and applies them to the atheist. He or she, like everyone else in history, has often cried, "That's not fair!" His or her atheism, in fact, rests in part upon the view that the present world is too unjust to attribute it to a loving God. And by leveling this accusation of unfairness, he or she implies that somewhere fairness exists. He or she, to avoid irrationality and self-refutation, must believe in a standard of justice which can be used as a point of reference. No one can claim anything to be unfair without fairness as its standard, any more that I can declare anything to be unequal to one foot without a ruler as my standard.

Point 1: Everyone in history has considered the universe to be
unfair.
Point 2: Everyone, then, must concede that fairness also exists.
Point 3: The atheist is no exception.

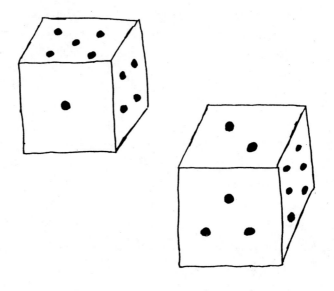

100% chance

Figure 33:
The Universe of the Atheist

Day 33
the atheist's ambiguity regarding justice (I)

"Thus, in the very act of trying to prove that God did not exist–in other words, that the whole of reality was senseless–I found I was forced to assume that one part of reality–namely my idea of justice–was full of sense. Consequently, atheism turns out to be too simple."

- former atheist C. S. LEWIS

To expose the hypocrisy of the atheist, consider the following:

You and I decide to spend some time on a rainy day playing a dice game. We take turns rolling the dice and see who rolls the highest number. Every time you roll a higher number than I do, I give you a dollar bill. Every time I roll higher, you place a buck in my hands. After 100 rolls, it just so happens that I have had to give you $75, and you have had to give me $25. Incredibly, the dice have landed in your favor three-fourths of the time. Would I consider this to be unfair? No, I would not, for the simple reason that the whole exercise was one of pure chance. It was luck (good for you and bad for me) and nothing else that tipped the scales in your favor. Even if I was poor and needed the money and you were rich and didn't, I still could not cry, "That's not fair!" The truth is that there is no such thing as fairness and unfairness in a world of 100% chance. There is only a mixture of good luck and bad luck, good fortune and bad fortune.

Atheists look at the universe much like the dice shoot above. They see it to be the product of blind evolutionary forces, 100% the result of chance. Everything that happens within it is labeled by them as fortunate or unfortunate, good luck or bad luck. They will not admit anything to be fair or unfair. No such thing as fairness and unfairness can exist, they say, in a universe of pure chance. Things may be advantageous or not advantageous to the individual, but they cannot be considered to be just or unjust. Atheists believe that justice is a myth, right and wrong a matter of personal taste. They, like C. S. Lewis in his atheist days, project to us a "senseless" world devoid of absolute meaning, purpose, justice, or morality.

The problem is that they don't live what they believe. If they truly believe the universe to be 100% chance, they would never shout, "That's not fair!" But, as we have noted earlier, they do shout it. If they truly believe that justice is a myth, they would consider the cruelty meted out to them by the world to be bad luck and move on. But they don't just accept the bad and move on. If they really believe what they are saying, they would say the universe has rolled them a series of low numbers and would write it off as such. But they do not write it off. They should, like I did above, resign themselves to the fact that it is just their bad luck that they are poor, sick, and weak and just their neighbor's good luck that he is rich, healthy, and powerful. But they don't resign themselves to this fact.

Let me remind you of Lenin and Stalin, two of the most passionate revolutionaries in recent history, and of Karl Marx, their philosophical mentor. They all were staunch atheists. We would have expected them to take what the universe dished out. They did just the opposite. While denying that the universe had any justice, they proceeded to legislate their own in violent passion.

Figure 34:
The Ambiguity of the Atheist Concerning Morality/Justice

Day 34
the atheist's ambiguity regarding justice (II)

*"The modern age, more or less repudiating the idea of
a divine lawgiver, has nevertheless tried to retain the
ideas of moral right and wrong..."*

- ethicist RICHARD TAYLOR

We can better see the inconsistency of the atheist's position if
we go back to our game of dice. What if you and I play the same
game and once again (what rotten luck!) you have $75 and I have
$25 after a hundred rolls. This time, however, I discover that you
are using dice that are weighted–making it more likely for you to
roll a higher number–and I am using regular dice. Would I brush
this off as easily as yesterday? Of course, not! I would accuse you
of unfair tactics and demand my money back immediately. If you
reply that the game remains a game of chance and allude to the $25
in my hand as evidence that it is still possible for me to roll a higher
number, I would not be amused. I would say to you that you have
chosen to stack the odds in your favor, that though the game still
depends on the luck of the roll of the dice, it is not a fair game by
any standards. If you refuse to give me the money back, I would be
infuriated and would take measures to correct the injustice. If it is
true that you are rich and don't need the money and I am poor and
do, my fury would be even hotter and my quest for justice more
intense.

Atheists would like us to believe that the world is 100% chance
and that no such thing as fairness or unfairness exists. They do
not tend to act, however, as if this is true. Instead, when atheists
look around the world and see how others have chosen to stack the
odds against them, they immediately begin to think it all unfair.
Even if they are told they still have a chance–albeit a slim one–to
succeed, they are not amused. They still demand the playing field

to be leveled. If not, they threaten to level it themselves. Isn't that what Lenin and Stalin did? Didn't they, like all atheists, act on the assumption that life was not fair?

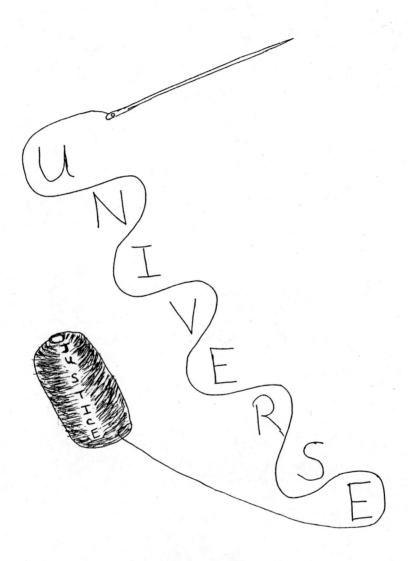

Figure 35:

The Spool of Justice

Day 35
the Moral Law within us

"... the requirements of the law are written on their hearts ..."

- PAUL, the apostle

We have now come full-circle in our *Argument from Fairness.* We have noted that everyone, including the atheist, has tended to look at life and cry, "That's not fair!" We have seen that if such unfairness exists in the universe, then fairness (a system of justice) must also exist as well. We have observed how inconsistent and hypocritical the atheist appears, at one moment alleging that this chance universe has no sense of justice, no absolute right or wrong, then the next moment proclaiming—as he retaliates against people who have stacked the odds against him—that it's his absolute right to do so.

The atheist, you see, wants to have his cake and eat it, too. He wants to say that there is no such thing as fairness in the world, but he wants to live as if there is. In fact, it is my assertion that he is forced to live that way, for that's the way the universe is made. It is a universe with a thread of justice run through it. Only when the atheist sees this will he realize that the very way he looks at the universe, the whole foundation of his atheism, is wrong.

Contrast this with the person who believes in God. He or she believes that God the Designer created this universe and imposed upon it His own sense of justice and morality. When things appear unjust, the theist can say, "That's not fair!," and not be called a hypocrite. When people act badly, he or she can say, "That's not right!," and not be considered inconsistent. He or she believes that fairness exists in the universe and that the existence of God is the only explanation for it. The theist believes that all human beings have a God-given sense of right and wrong, a Moral Law, "written on their hearts."

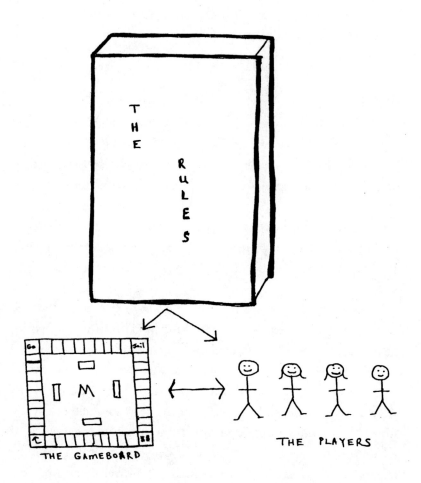

Figure 36:

The Relationship Between the Rules and the Game

Day 36
Point Four: justice must come from God

"Ethics, if it is anything, is supernatural."

- philosopher LUDWIG WITTGENSTEIN

The fourth and final point of the *Argument from Fairness* is that justice and morality, if they exist, must come from God. The best way to look at this is to consider the whole matter of rules. If you think about it, you will see that rules always transcend the game itself. They are essential to the game but cannot be equal to the game. Take, for example, the rules of Monopoly. They cannot be the same as the game pieces or the game board. They must be separate from them, in a sense *above and beyond* them. The rules likewise cannot be the Monopoly players themselves but must be a separate entity to which these opponents can refer. The rules of football are the same. Sanctioned by the league officials, embraced by the players and coaches, and upheld by the referees, they must by their very nature transcend the component parts of the game. It is this way in music as well. The keyboard is the playing field, the keys the game pieces, and the pianist the player. The notes on the sheet of music are the rules. These notes are separate from the keyboard and keys and from the pianist, who must follow them if music is to be played.

To summarize, the keyboard, keys, and pianist cannot be a part of the sheet of music; the latter transcends the former. The playing field, goalposts, and quarterback cannot be a part of the rules. The rules of football must be separate and transcending. In similar fashion, the rules of Monopoly must be separate and distinct from the board, game pieces, and players.

Now nature is the "field" upon which the "game of life" is played, and we are the "players" of the game. If there are rules of justice that govern life, then these rules–for the reasons just stated—must be transcendent. They must be separate and distinct from *nature* (the "field") and must be separate and distinct from *humanity* (the "players"). They cannot, therefore, be attributed (as atheists are prone to say) to *natural* instincts or *human* opinion. And since these rules of life must transcend both nature and us, they must (by the process of elimination) be supernatural in origin. In other words, *the Moral Law must come from God.* Fairness and justice (which include right and wrong and the rules that govern them) must arise from a source that is transcendent, *above and beyond* nature and man. Its source must be of supernatural origin. Its source must be God Himself.[1]

The conclusion here is that justice, if it exists at all, must have come from God. It could not have any other origin. The only question that remains is whether or not justice exists, and we have already proven how silly the atheist looks when he or she says it doesn't.

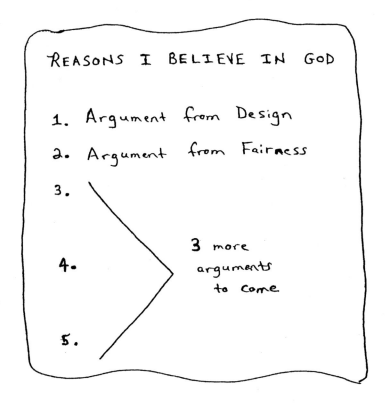

Figure 37:

Where We've Been and Where We're Going

Day 37
the first two arguments reviewed

"The issue is whether the world is explicable solely in terms of itself, i.e. is the world itself ultimate, or is there a being other than the world to which the world is related?"

- philosopher DAVID H. FREEMAN

Before we proceed to my third argument for the existence of God, let's pause and summarize the two we have examined thus far. The first, usually referred to as the *Argument from Design,* focuses on the obvious design present in the universe and infers from it the existence of an Intelligent Designer. The strength of this argument, we have seen, is its simplicity and its appeal to common sense, for hardly anyone has a problem understanding that there must be a creator (for example, a watchmaker) behind an organized structure (in this case, a watch). The only recourse for the atheist is to assert that the universe is either eternal or illusory (and, therefore, in no need of a Creator) or to try to divert attention from the subject at hand by pointing to the presence in the universe of evil, pain, and suffering, all of which call into question God's character, not His existence.

The second defense, what I call the *Argument from Fairness,* emphasizes the tendency every person has to designate things as fair/unfair and right/wrong. It asserts that such a sense of justice and morality must originate from a source *above and beyond* nature, a supernatural source. It likens the rules of right and wrong to the notes on a sheet of music, giving the "pianist" (humanity) directions on how to behave on the "keyboard" (earth). The atheist responds by saying that there is no such thing as fair/unfair and right/wrong in a universe that is, as he believes it to be, based on pure chance. The problem is that he does not act consistent with his worldview.

In fact, when confronted with life's misfortunes, he is quick to call his lot unfair and his cause right. Atheists, therefore, attempt to deny the universe any justice and morality and then try to impose on the universe their own brand of each. The contradiction here between thought and practice is blatantly obvious.

The simplest deductions from the two arguments above would be:

1. that the presence of design in the universe demands the existence of a supernatural Designer; and
2. that the presence of fairness/morality (i.e. a Moral Law) in the universe demands the existence of a supernatural Lawgiver.

These are the conclusions I and a multitude of others, many former atheists, have reached on our religious journeys. If you are not yet convinced, perhaps the next argument will compel you to join us.

the **Argument from Supernatural Belief**

Figure 38:

The Blind Man Discovers That Darkness Is Not All There Is

Day 38
outside help (I)

> *"The direct inference from black to white...staggers belief."*

> - apologist C. S. LEWIS

To begin the next argument, imagine with me a person blind since birth who has lived his entire life alone on a deserted island. Having been left there as an infant, he has never heard that light exists and has never seen one glimmer of it. As far as he is concerned, the world is complete darkness upon which is superimposed a mixture of sounds, smells, and sensations. The man, having no idea that light exists, does not long for it one bit. He assumes that darkness is ultimate reality. He has no reason to assume otherwise.

Now answer this question: is it possible for this man, unless he has *outside help,* to begin to believe in the existence of light and to reverence it as something worthy to attain? The obvious answer is that it is not possible without such help, because the concept of light is completely foreign to his view of the world. He has no idea that light exists, is not looking for it, and cannot perceive it. It is, therefore, impossible for him to begin to believe in it unless someone or something outside himself informs him of its existence. Perhaps a boat lands one day on his island and its passengers tell him of a world never dreamed of, a world of visual perception– rainbows and sunsets, moonlight and stars, reflections of others in the sun's glow and of himself in the water's surface. Perhaps he is informed of the possibility of light by a bird or monkey or some other nonhuman element of the natural world. Or maybe a spirit or a ghost or a god decides to place in his mind the novel idea that light exists and, in so doing, begins this man's quest amidst the darkness of his life to find it. Better still, this supernatural being might actually bestow upon him the gift of sight and let him perceive the reality of light firsthand. Regardless, the point here remains the same. This man begins to believe in light only because the seed of awareness has first been planted within him from an outside source.

Although hypothetical, this picture of a blind man completely unaware of the existence of light is easy for all of us to grasp. It is likewise easy for us to see that unless he has *outside help,* light would never enter his mind. We all can understand that the idea of light must be put into his mind by something or someone within nature (other humans, for example) or by something or someone outside of nature (for example, God). Without such outside intervention, light could be all around him in its most radiant and awe-inspiring forms, and he would remain oblivious to it. He would not sense it, desire it, or seek it. Neither would we, were we placed in the same predicament.

The relevance of this to our discussion of God's existence is enormous and will be explained in detail in the next days ahead. Before turning the page, however, I would ask you to review today's illustration once more to make sure that you understand it and accept it as true.

Species: Cave Fish   Species: Ocean-Bottom Fish

Environment: Darkness (100%)   Environment: Water (100%)

Awareness
of
Light :   None

Awareness
of
Ocean Surface :   None

Figure 39:
**Two Fish Trapped Within Their
Environments**

Day 39
outside help (II)

"...it is incongruous with everything else we know about the world to suppose that nature could produce creatures which have longings which nature doesn't itself fulfill."

- apologist GREGORY A. BOYD

Yesterday's illustration of the blind man on a deserted island has a counterpart in the animal world that may serve to reinforce it. I remember as a child visiting several caves with my parents and recall listening to a guide tell us about some unique fish deep within it. The novelty about these fish was that they were completely blind. Although possessing eyes, years of nonuse in complete darkness had rendered them nonfunctional. I recall how amazed I was when the guide beamed a bright flashlight into the waters and the fish acted as if nothing had changed. In a very real sense, they were like our blind friend, unaware of the existence of light and unaffected by its presence all around them. Ignorant of its existence, they could not feel the slightest hint of being disabled. They could not possess the first inkling to desire it or pursue it unless they were first informed of its possibility. Something or someone would have to somehow plant the idea of light in them; otherwise, nothing would change. To get to know light, they must be made aware of it, and for this they would have to rely on an outside source.

Other examples could be cited that confirm this principle. Take, for example, those bottom-dwelling fish swimming miles under the ocean's surface, never knowing anything else but water all around them. They would not consider themselves to be wet, for they have no idea what dry is. To them, total immersion is ultimate reality. To make these creatures aware of the world above would require outside intervention, such as a free ride to the surface from underwater explorers. Only with such *outside help* could they get a glimpse of the upper world and begin to experience it as a reality.

Now humans throughout history have possessed the notion that something supernatural exists. As far back as archaeology can unearth, belief in a supernatural world has been a universal finding. How is it possible for this thought to creep into the collective consciousness of humanity, and what does this have to do with the fish and the blind man alluded to above? Tomorrow we will attempt to supply the answers.

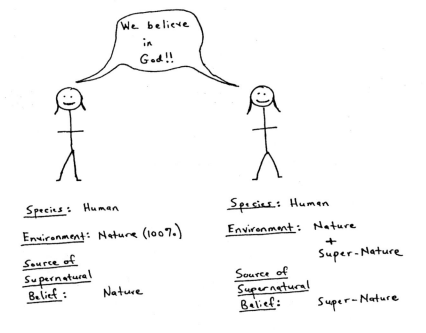

Figure 40:

The Atheistic (L) and Theistic (R) Explanations of Supernatural Belief

Day 40
the argument defined

> *"If there isn't a natural explanation and there doesn't seem to be the potential for finding one, then I believe it's appropriate to look at a supernatural explanation."*

> \- scientist WALTER L. BRADLEY

Let me state three facts, two agreed upon by the atheist and a third with which he will argue:

1. Atheists believe that the natural world is all there is, that there is no such reality that can be described as supernatural.
2. From the earliest recorded history to today, human beings have tended to believe that such a supernatural reality exists.
3. Awareness of the supernatural could not be present in the human mind unless it was planted by a supernatural source.

You will see I am right if you take the first two facts above and try to reconcile them from the atheistic viewpoint. Atheists believe that the natural world is all there is. To them, there is no other reality. They believe that men and women are 100% natural creatures, as completely surrounded by nature as the blind man and cave fish were by darkness. If so, you would expect humans, like the blind man and the fish, to be unaware of anything outside their immediate experience. You certainly would not expect such men and women—unless they had *outside help*—to acknowledge, desire, or reverence anything supernatural any more than you expected the blind man or the cave fish on their own to acknowledge, desire, or reverence light. You would not expect humans, if as immersed in nature as the ocean-bottom fish were in water, to ever conceive on their own the possibility of a supernatural world "above."

But what you have throughout history are men and women doing just that. On the earliest pottery pieces unearthed by archaeologists, on the most primitive cave drawings deciphered to date, and within the first pyramidal royal tombs explored in Egypt, evidence abounds of a belief in—almost an obsession with—the supernatural, one that has continued unabated to the present. What you have in history are people, supposedly engulfed in nothing but nature, believing that something more than nature exists.

As with the blind man and the fish, such a leap of knowledge and awareness could never have occurred without *outside help*. Something or someone had to alert humanity that the supernatural was possible; if not, we would never have fathomed it in the least. The question is: who or what brought it to our attention? Atheists would say that this intervening agent, this voice directing man to begin to look outside nature, came from within nature itself. But this is, at best, inconsistent with their worldview. If nature is all there is, as atheists are so apt to remind us, it is hardly believable that it could relay to mankind the idea that something *supra*-natural, something outside itself, exists. But if not from nature, then from whence did man's supernatural awareness come? As long as my mind is allowed to reflect on it, I cannot come up with any other candidate than something supernatural itself. It must have been a spirit, a ghost, or (could it be?) a God, all of them supernatural, that gave to men and women this odd sense that nature is not the end. It must have come from beyond nature, this novel idea put into our collective consciousness that a supernatural world exists as real as the natural. It must have been something or someone separate from nature that planted this seed within us and started us on our individual quests to nourish and harvest it. It must be that same supernatural voice that entices men and women today to seek Him until they find Him.

This, my third argument for God's existence, is what I refer to as the *Argument from Supernatural Belief.* Stated simply, it claims that *belief in the supernatural could never have happened without **outside help**, unless a supernatural source intervened to make us aware of its existence.*[1]

Figure 41:
A Baffling Paradox

Day 41
a "good" God in a "bad" world

"There was one question which I never dreamed of raising…If the universe is so bad, or even half so bad, how on earth did human beings ever come to attribute it to the activity of a wise and good Creator?"

- former atheist C. S. LEWIS

The *Argument from Supernatural Belief* focuses on the overwhelming consensus throughout history that the supernatural exists and argues that such a belief could have arisen only if that supernatural reality let us in on its secret. It states that nature alone could not possibly have been the author of our awareness of things beyond nature, just as an atlas of North America alone could not be the source of our awareness of things in the southern hemisphere. Belief in the supernatural, therefore, implies and demands the existence of the supernatural itself.

What is even more astounding about all this is the tendency through the ages to ascribe to this supernatural reality a benevolent disposition. It is one thing, a distance we cannot ourselves jump, to go from a worldview limited to nature to one that includes both nature and the supernatural. That is evidence enough that the supernatural is real. It is another thing, a leap of equal magnitude, to possess a belief in the cruelty of nature and then begin to believe the supernatural anything but cruel. This is not at all what you would expect in a world considered so bad and impersonal. Such a realization–that the supernatural is good–could not have come from nature or have been deduced from nature any more than belief in the supernatural itself could have a natural origin. It, too, must have come from elsewhere, specifically from God.

The atheist keeps reminding us *ad nauseam* of the disorder and chaos in the universe and tells us there is no way he or she can attribute this to a loving God. The remarkable thing to remember is that the majority of mankind has disagreed. They have come to the baffling conclusion that behind nature's apparent injustice and malevolence is a just and benevolent Spirit. Somehow the atheist must explain this paradox. He may say that humans have deduced this from nature itself, but this would go against his basic view of nature as cruel. Or he may claim that humanity's belief in a loving God originated from outside nature, but then he will be admitting that there is more to reality than nature itself. The atheist, then, has painted himself into a corner. There is for him no logical escape.

Figure 42:
The Atheist's Rebuttal

Day 42
the atheist's rebuttal

*"I do not believe in a God. The belief in a God is still
generally accepted... But, in the light of scientific
discoveries and demonstrations, such a belief is
unfounded and untenable today."*

- British atheist ROBERT BLATCHFORD

We have noted that belief in a supernatural reality is uniform across contemporary and ancient cultures, and we have surmised that the very presence of this belief puts the atheist in a very real dilemma. How did such a belief come to be? We have answered that it must have been placed within our minds by the supernatural itself, that it would be impossible for nature—if nature is all there is—to introduce something to us outside of the natural realm. Not to be outdone, the atheist will usually counter with an alternate explanation for our supernatural belief. In summary form, it goes like this:

Primitive man, ignorant of the physics of the natural world around him yet dependent upon nature for his very existence, began to either reverence or fear its component parts. The sun, for example, became an object of favor and wind and locusts objects of disfavor. Man then began to believe that he could influence these natural objects through rituals or behaviors. Thus was born religion, a projection of man's hopes and fears regarding the natural world. Later men and women took this primitive nature religion and, as scientific advances shed light on their world, began to project their hopes and fears to sources more transcendent than before. Still, the universal belief in the supernatural remains today nothing more than our response to nature itself. It is our futile attempt to woo nature's benefits and deflect its fury. If the truth were known, it serves no useful purpose other than to appease us in our ignorance. Sooner or later, with the continued march of science, it will be discarded once and for all.

Now I agree with the atheist up to a certain point. Primitive man did fear and favor the component parts of nature around him and did begin to try to influence them through rituals. I agree that it was futile for him to do so, for we all know that ritualistic fervor, no matter how sincere, will not change the course of the sun in the sky or send rain upon a parched earth. The activity of the sun and the excesses and shortages of precipitation are now known to be governed by scientific laws unknown to early man. I agree that modern science has made nature religion obsolete, reserved only for those who are scientifically illiterate.

Where I disagree with the atheist is his assertion that today's religions are essentially grown-up versions of these primitive religions, that the former are a continuation of the latter. I do not believe that nature religion, worship solely directed toward nature itself, could have ever given birth to modern religions like Judaism or Christianity that worship a transcendent God, preeminent and preexistent to nature.

Tomorrow I will use an illustration that may help us see more clearly the error of the atheist's argument.

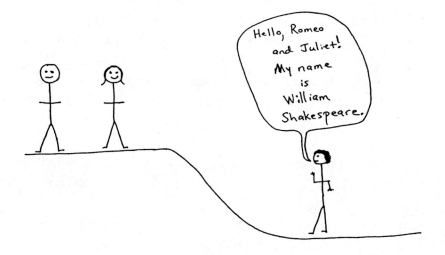

Figure 43:
Romeo and Juliet Meet Their Creator

Day 43
outside help (III)

"The fool says in his heart, 'There is no God!'"

- the PSALMIST

We are all familiar with the fictional characters Romeo and Juliet. Set in Italy centuries ago, their story of love in the face of adversity remains a touching classic today. For the purpose of our discussion, I want you to consider what reality is to Romeo and Juliet. What do they perceive to be their world? If you think about it a while, you will come to the conclusion that the entire extent of their reality is the play itself. They know nothing except what the storyline dictates. They know each other and any other character they happen to meet in the play but cannot be aware of anyone outside it. They know all the settings in the play wherein they are placed but cannot possibly know other settings. They can acknowledge, adore, loathe, and reverence anyone or anything included in the plot but cannot acknowledge, adore, loathe, or reverence anyone or anything outside it. Their entire reality is confined to the storyline itself. It is impossible for them to perceive anything else.

Atheists argue that nature is the only reality and that you and I act out our lives totally within its confines. In their opinion, nature is the storyline, and we are the characters. They believe that we, like Romeo and Juliet, can acknowledge, adore, loathe, and reverence anything within our storyline. We can reverence nature and seek its benefits, just as Romeo and Juliet began to love each other and seek ways to fulfill that love. In fact, this is exactly what nature religions are. They, say the atheists, are expressions of mankind's reverence of nature and of his desire to influence it in his favor. Their existence can be explained without having to believe at all in a supernatural world.

Up to this point, I think the atheist is right. Pure nature religions, ritual and worship directed at natural objects, need no other explanation than nature itself for their existence in men's minds. We do not have to believe in a supernatural reality to account for them. Where I think the atheist is mistaken can be seen by looking again at Romeo and Juliet. What if these two characters in the play suddenly began to believe that something or someone *outside* the storyline existed? What if they began to believe, for example, that someone named William Shakespeare existed and that he was the creator of them and the world around them? Would it be possible, without *outside help*, for them to acknowledge, adore, loathe, or reverence him? No, it would not! In fact, the only way they could come to know about William Shakespeare is for Shakespeare himself to let them know. He could have inserted an additional character into the play and added a scene where that character tells Romeo and Juliet of his existence. Or he could have written himself into the play, making himself one of the characters, and scripted himself to walk right up to the two lovebirds and say, "Hi! My name is William Shakespeare. In my writing room at home, I created you and your world." In that way, too, the idea of another world—a reality outside the play itself, the creative world of William Shakespeare—could have entered their minds. It could never have happened, however, unless William Shakespeare put it there. Even the possibility of his existence could never have entered their minds unless he did.

So it is with religion today. Atheists may claim until they are blue in the face that nature religions gave birth to Judaism, Christianity, and Islam, but what they are shouting still won't make sense to me. To say that we have come to believe in God through nature alone, totally without any *outside help*, is like saying that Romeo and Juliet could come to know Shakespeare without Shakespeare's help. How could men and women living in a world 100% natural ever come to believe that something beyond nature exists? How could they begin to believe that a God in heaven created them and their world? How could nature or religions spawned by nature ever be responsible for the belief that exists today in a supernatural God? The only logical answer is this: our supernatural awareness would never have happened unless God Himself "wrote it into the script." Without His help, even the possibility of His existence would never have entered our minds.[1]

Figure 44:
The Ancients Learn About God

Day 44
divine education

"...the God beyond the mountain, the God beyond the sky... This God is the initiator; he encounters [human beings], they do not encounter him."

- author THOMAS CAHILL

I want to add something at this point about those primitive nature religions. The atheist seems to assume that they consisted only of nature worship, that none of them had any notion of a reality beyond nature. But is this true? One look inside the pyramids of Egypt will show you that it is not. There you will find the mummies of Egyptian royalty entombed with their kingly possessions and their servants. Obviously they are anticipating life after death, a journey beyond the grave to another world, a world beyond nature, one that looks very much supernatural. This same supernatural thread can be found in Sumer and Babylon and other ancient cultures. That the worship of nature can be found in all of them cannot be disputed, but these appear to be nature religions into which a hint of the supernatural is woven. If this is true, we have already concluded that nature could not be the seamstress sewing this supernatural thread. The weaver must also be supernatural.

It seems, then, that even in these primitive nature religions the voice of God can be heard, telling the ancients there is more to reality than nature alone. In the Babylonian *Epic of Gilgamesh* and in other extant writings in ancient languages like Sumerian cuneiform and Egyptian hieroglyphics, occasional odd and curious references to a world outside nature can be found, references that are inexplicable unless something outside of nature is letting these early writers sense its existence. What you see here, in my opinion, is the beginning of man's education about God by God. Like a teacher showing first-graders the existence of an alphabet, God begins with man at the most rudimentary level, the level of nature worship, and inserts there the ABCs of His existence. He takes man's myths and superstitions and uses them as a medium through which truth about Him can be grasped.

Thus we see in these nature religions the beginning of a journey that leads centuries later to the words of one considered by many to be God Himself: "You have heard that only on this mountain you should worship God. I say to you that God is a spirit and that anyone who worships Him must worship Him in spirit and in truth."[1] Words cannot relate how beautiful this whole process appears to all of us who worship God today.

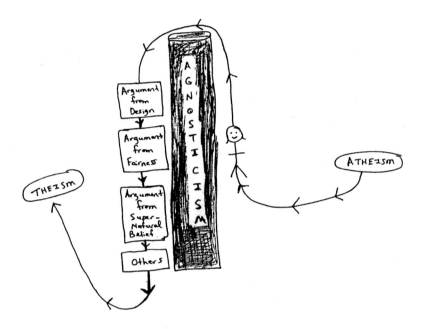

Figure 45:
The Weight of the Evidence

Day 45
a look back, a look ahead

"...I've tried to show he [God] exists by appealing to the common facts of science, ethics, history, and philosophy. Taken together, they form a powerful case for God..."

- theologian/philosopher WILLIAM LANE CRAIG

It is now over six weeks since our journey began. Along the way we have looked at three arguments for the existence of God. As your guide, I have challenged you to look at the world around you and explain how certain things came to be. What is the best explanation for the universe's design? How can you account for the sense of fairness that resides in mankind? Why is there this tendency through the ages to acknowledge a supernatural world? The answer to each question has been the same: the existence of God is the best explanation.

We must now take broader and quicker steps. There are two more reasons to believe in God still to be considered. We will add these to the *Argument from Design*, the *Argument from Fairness*, and the *Argument from Supernatural Belief* and thus bring the first leg of our pilgrimage to a close. By then, the choice between theism and atheism should be easier for you. If you have not already done so, you should be persuaded by the weight of the evidence to get off the fence and to point the compass of your heart in the direction of God.

The **Argument from Human Characteristics**

Figure 46:

The Argument from Human Characteristics

Day 46
the argument defined

"If the ultimate canvas against which the cosmos is painted is not personal like we are, then we are very much like fish out of water."

— apologist GREGORY A. BOYD

Suppose that you and I are invited to a friend's house for coffee and dessert. Upon entering the house, we are escorted into his dining room and asked to have a seat. Seconds later our friend returns from the kitchen with three cups of freshly brewed coffee and three slices of homemade chocolate pie. He informs us that he prepared the coffee and the pie in his kitchen just before our arrival. If he is telling the truth, you and I can look at the drink and dessert before us and know in part what his kitchen is like. Even without stepping one foot into it, we can be certain that it contains an oven or microwave, because the first bites of pie we put into our mouths are warm. We know instantly that it has a refrigerator to keep the cream in our coffee cold and the eggs in the meringue topping fresh. We also correctly assume that the kitchen has utensils to stir coffee with, pans to pour chocolate filling into, and spices that give flavor to both. We can say all this without hesitation, because we know that any characteristic of the coffee and chocolate pie must be present in the kitchen in which they were made. In fact, if the pie is hot and our friend tells us his kitchen has no heating appliance, we would say to him that it cannot be a product of his kitchen alone. We know that everything made exclusively in that kitchen must be able to be explained by it.

Now suppose that you and I later attend a banquet and begin to converse with several people at our table. As we get to know each other, we find that we have several characteristics in common. We each have "a mind that is self-aware and rational, a heart which is free and can love and which is, therefore, morally responsible, and a soul (or call it what you will) which longs for meaning and significance." Just as sure as we described the chocolate pie as warm and the coffee as spicy, we determine that everyone at our table has these characteristics: rationality, morality, and purpose.

Having made these observations, we turn our attention to the guest speaker at the banquet. He introduces himself as an atheist and begins to explain his view of the world. During his speech, he quotes existentialist atheist Jean-Paul Sartre: "It is meaningless that we are born; it is meaningless that we die." Then he quotes atheist Sigmund Freud: "The moment a man questions the meaning and value of life, he is sick, since objectively neither has any existence." He goes on to express the unanimous opinion of atheists by describing the universe as irrational, amoral, and purposeless.

When he is finished and the floor is opened for questions, you immediately stand to your feet and begin to speak:

> Sir, this afternoon I enjoyed coffee and pie prepared in my friend's kitchen. The pie was warm and the coffee spicy, so I knew that the kitchen had to have warmth and spices within it. I knew that anything that came from his kitchen must be explained by it. But what you are telling me tonight about the universe is just the opposite. I am surrounded at my table by men and women who are rational, moral, and purposeful. That we are all products of nature and nature alone you boldly proclaim. Then you turn around and say that nature itself, the "kitchen" from which we are made, has no reason or morals or purpose. You are claiming that nature has produced humans with characteristics that it does not possess itself. How, sir, is this possible? If nature has no reason, morals, and purpose and humans do, doesn't it mean that these traits must have originated somewhere else than nature? Doesn't this prove that something other than nature is out there, that a supernatural "kitchen" must exist to explain these characteristics we share? Doesn't the existence of these personal traits in a world considered devoid of them demand the existence of God?

You then sit down, having just voiced my fourth argument

for God's existence, what I call the *Argument from Human Characteristics.*

Figure 47:
How Can This Be?

Day 47
multiple questions, one answer

"Man cannot find the ultimate expression of his own being anywhere but in God Himself."

- philosopher EDWARD SILLEM

The *Argument from Human Characteristics* states that several human traits cannot be accounted for unless they have a supernatural source. It is a broader version of the *Argument from Fairness* and the *Argument from Supernatural Belief* and, like them, tries to explain the characteristics humanity as a whole possesses. It comes to the same conclusion of the preceding arguments (that nature alone cannot be responsible) and points toward the same solution (the reality of God).

Let's make a running list of human characteristics that the atheist, given his view of the world, has a hard time explaining. In question form, they are as follows:

-If the universe is irrational and we are rational, what is the source of our rationality?

-If the universe is amoral and we are moral beings, where did our sense of right and wrong originate?

-If the universe is purposeless and we believe there is a purpose to our lives, from whence did our sense of purpose come?

-If the universe has no sense of fairness and justice and we do, how did we obtain it?

-If the universe has no meaning and we perceive meaning in our lives, how did we find it?

-If the universe is not self-aware and we are, where did we attain consciousness?

-If the universe has no love and we do, how do we explain the feeling of love within us?

-If the universe has no controlling mind and we do, how did we come to possess it?

-If the universe is impersonal and we are personal, what is the source of our personhood?

-If the universe has no God and we believe He exists, how did we become aware of Him?

Remember that even an atheistic skeptic like David Hume (Day 14's quotation) knew that every effect must have a cause. To be consistent, then, atheists must be able to explain how nature—to them, the one and only cause—can produce characteristics in its creatures that it doesn't itself possess. To put it bluntly, I don't believe they can. If we remember this commonsense principle of cause and effect, the summary answer to the questions above is that all of these human characteristics (rationality, morality, purpose, fairness and justice, meaning, consciousness, love, cognition, and personality) must have come from something that is rational, moral, purposeful, fair and just, meaningful, self-aware, loving, cognizant, and personal. It appears that there is a force behind the universe that is beginning to look less and less like the "blind force" of nature and more and more like a real God. And it begins to look this way because it makes the most sense to us, not just because we wish it to be so.[1]

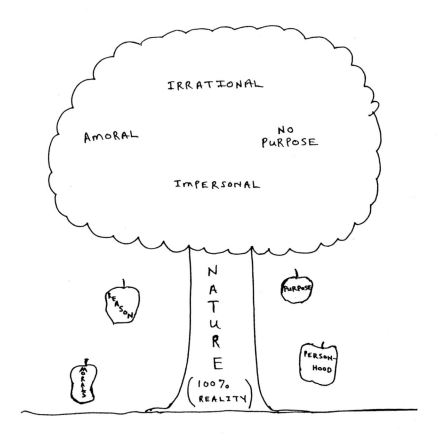

Figure 48:

Atheism – A Violation of the Principle of Cause and Effect

Day 48
cause and effect in the "backyard"

> *"The actual theory of atheism...entails at the close*
> *of the argument a manifest absurdity..."*

> - apologist ALPHONSE GRATY

Another way to see the truth of the *Argument from Human Characteristics* is to imagine walking through a backyard littered with apples. With apples everywhere at your feet, you don't have to look up to know that there is an apple tree nearby. You know that apples must come from apple trees, that an effect must be able to be explained by its cause.

What if you also encountered a few oranges in the same yard? Would you assume these to have come from the apple tree, too? No, you would immediately surmise that they came from somewhere else, specifically from an orange tree. To say that the apple tree could produce oranges goes against all you know about the world. You know that the presence of the oranges has to be explained by a reality other than the apple tree. Any other assertion would be laughable and indefensible.

But this is just what the atheist is asserting. He first claims the entire universe to be irrational, amoral, and without purpose. Then, as he walks through the universe's "backyard" and sees at his feet human "fruits" like reason, morality, and purpose, he still denies the existence of any "tree" other than nature. He asks us to believe that nature can produce "fruit" incompatible with itself, that it is irrational but can produce rational humans, that it is amoral but can produce moral humans, that it is without purpose but can produce purposeful humans. What he asks us to believe does not make sense. If nature does not possess these characteristics and we do, we all know that there must be a "tree" other than nature in the universe's "backyard." In addition to nature, there must be a reality that is rational and moral and purposeful. We know a supernatural source must exist as soon as we see these "fruit" within us, for the same reason we know an orange tree must exist as soon as we see oranges at our feet.

Reason, morality, and purpose in human beings...

A. really do not exist.

B. come from our animal instincts..

C. are offset by humanity's irrationality,
    immorality, and purposeless actions.

Figure 49:
The Atheist Responds to the Argument from Human Characteristics

Day 49
the atheist's rebuttal

"Doesn't evolutionary theory say that our minds and morality are just a part of our survival drive?"

- EDWARD K. BOYD, to his Christian son

If atheists are adamant that the universe has no reason, morals, and purpose, how do they explain the presence of these characteristics in humanity as a whole without having to admit the existence of God? How do they answer the *Argument from Human Characteristics*?

One way is to try to deny that humans have these characteristics at all. The appearance of reason, morality, and purpose in human beings could be just that—only an appearance. If the truth were known, some atheists claim, these traits are not what they seem to be. They are not real, and the fact that they are not means that no supernatural entity is needed to explain them. Nature thus remains the one and only reality.

The problem with this line of thinking is that it goes completely against what atheists observe in the world on a daily basis. They deny the existence of human reason, morality, and purpose while humans that appear rational, moral, and purposeful are walking all around them. They ask us to look in the mirror and deny that we have any of these traits then expect us to accept their ideas as rational and their outlook meaningful. They claim that what they observe all around them and within them is only a mirage, an illusion. At its core, this answer to the *Argument from Human Characteristics* is just another version of the illusory theory used by atheists to discredit the *Argument from Design*. It falls short of its goal for the same reason: it doesn't hold true in real life.

Another way to discredit the *Argument from Human Characteristics* is to say that our sense of reason, morality, and purpose is a product of our animal instincts. Just as a dog at times appears to be smart or good but is acting only on instinct, reason and morality in humans could be nothing more than these same instincts evolutionally grown-up. Since our animal instincts come from nature, there then would be no need to look elsewhere to explain these characteristics. There would be no need to resort to supernatural belief.

The problem here is twofold. For one thing, this line of thinking still attributes to creatures of nature traits that nature itself does not possess. Nature, still considered an irrational and amoral "tree," is said to yield through its animal instincts rational and moral "fruit." The inconsistency of the atheist is not really changed. Secondly, the fact that we often are forced to choose one instinct (such as compassion) over another one (such as self-preservation) means that something more than our instincts must be at work. You cannot use another instinct to decide between the two any more than another key on the piano can decide for you which one of two keys you are to play. That decision must come from *above,* from the sheet of music (in the case of the pianist) and from the supernatural (in the case of humanity).[1]

The third way that atheists attempt to counter the *Argument from Human Characteristics* is to bring to our attention all the negative traits of man. Instead of focusing on humanity's tendency to love, reason, and act morally, they remind us that it is just as common for humans to hate, act irrationally, and be immoral. This, they say, is just as much evidence against the supernatural as the positive traits are evidence for it. The two cancel each other, leaving a stalemate.

What the atheist is attempting to do here, once again, is to distract us from the question at hand. That question does not concern any negative traits that humans happen to possess. (It is assumed that atheists, with such a negative worldview, can account for them.) The question at hand is whether or not atheists can explain the presence of positive human traits in a universe 100% negative, and the truth is that they cannot.

Very soon we will need to address the irrational and immoral side of humanity. It is a subject we cannot avoid, but it is one that should be reserved for the third leg of our journey, when the nature of humanity is explored. To point us in its direction now is just an attempt to evade the present issue.

Figure 50:
Atheistic Strategy – Evading the Main Issue

Day 50
the strategy of atheistic debate

"Atheism is a disease of the soul
before it is an error of the mind."

- PLATO

Let me add a few comments about atheistic arguments in general. There is a certain pattern to them. First, the atheist will attempt to provide rational reasons why he could be right and the theist wrong. This is what we saw yesterday in the first two rebuttals to the *Argument from Human Characteristics*. Then, when there is no rational answer or the ones available seem a bit far-fetched, atheists will try to distract the theist from the main issue. Questions will be raised by them that at first glance appear relevant to the subject at hand but on further reflection can be shown to be irrelevant. Yesterday's third answer of the atheist is a classic example. It is an attempt to divert us from the main subject, the presence of positive human traits, to another—the presence of negative ones. It is used, of course, because the atheist can explain the latter but cannot account for the former. The intention here is to get us off track, to divert our attention from the immediate road ahead. The theist must be alert to this tactic, recognize it when it comes, and expose it as nothing other than the atheist changing the subject.

Take, for example, the criticisms that the eighteenth century skeptic David Hume voiced concerning the *Argument from Design*.[1] When told that the universe, like a watch, must have a designer, he first tried to present rational alternatives. He argued that the universe could be more like a wild plant than a watch. Like the former, it could sprout on its own, show evidence of design, yet not require a designer. It could expand, then die, then sprout again, just as day lilies do year after year. What Hume was alluding to is a universe that needs no creator because that universe is eternal, forever recycling itself, forever expanding and contracting, forever creating itself anew. That this is a rational alternative to the *Argument from Design* has already been noted (Day 21), as has been the fact that it tends to conflict with recent scientific evidence pointing toward a finite universe.

If Hume had stopped there, he would have begun and ended on a rational note. But Hume did not stop there. He proceeded to resort to a diversionary tactic. He went on to argue that the universe, instead of being created by a great and perfect Intelligent Designer, might just as well have been the best effort of a committee of lesser gods or the first effort of a baby god. That this amounted to nothing more than changing the subject can be easily seen by all of us. Hume's assertion was an attempt to distract us from the subject at hand (whether a god exists) and redirect our focus to an entirely different subject (what this god is like). He conceded the existence of a designing force behind the universe then evaded the issue by calling into question the credentials of the designer(s). His response was no different than that of the young boy who, when caught with his hand in the cookie jar, tells his mother he intended to feed them to the dog. The boy's explanation does not in any way change the main issue (that his hand is in the jar); in fact, he concedes to her that it is. His statement to her is merely an attempt to distract her from that main issue. I doubt that he is successful. His mother is too smart to fall for that clever ploy. So should we be when the atheist, caught in a theological predicament, tries to evade the question at hand.

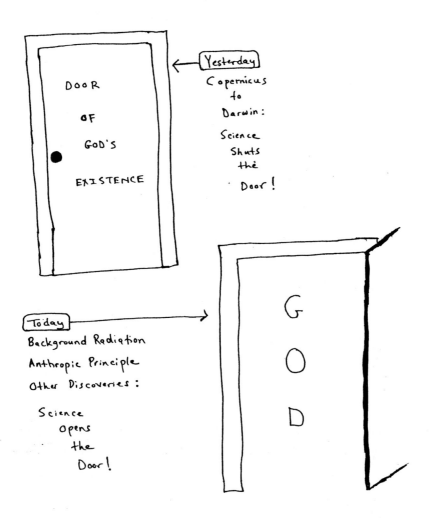

Figure 51:

Faith and Science –
Then and Now

Day 51
science and faith

"Late-twentieth-century science has overturned the assumptions that reigned at the end of the nineteenth century."

— scientist and Christian PATRICK GLYNN

Atheists have always tended to use discoveries of science as a weapon against theists. For a while, it appeared that they did so with good reason. Starting with Copernicus in the fifteenth century and continuing well into the twentieth, a succession of scientists painted a composite portrait of our universe that seemed quite different from the one traditionally described. The universe was not within our reach but was a vast expanse of mostly empty space, billions of light-years across, interspersed occasionally with stars and their planets. Earth was not the center of the universe, as had been touted for centuries, but turned out to be just another planet within it. Its claim to fame was that only on it (so far) had life been discovered. The world was not a few thousand years old, as creationists had claimed, but was found to extend much farther back in time than ever imagined. Man did not appear to be the most special creation on earth but the last in a long sequence of random evolutionary steps occurring totally within the natural world. Every stone scientists looked under seemed to yield something atheists could use as evidence and theists had to explain away. It was as if the door to God had been closed shut by science with no key available to humanity to reopen it.

The repercussions of all this in the last two centuries cannot be overstated. Belief in God, once taken for granted, has lost considerable ground to disbelief, especially in the scientific community. Although the great majority of Americans still believes that God exists, they are often perceived by the educated to do so out of scientific ignorance. Even among these "uninformed" masses, enough scientific information has become known to them to shake many a faith at its foundation. If theists are honest enough to admit it (very few are), at least a seed of doubt has been planted in many of their minds. Atheists, on the other hand, have tended to walk with a swagger. They have boldly asserted that the universe is 100% natural, that belief in God has become obsolete. The cry "God is dead!" has echoed through college campuses and has received considerable ink in the lay press. Along with the announcement of God's demise, the atheists have injected into the vacuum thus formed their own worldview, one that is devoid of any absolute morals, any sense of meaning and purpose, and any hope of life beyond the grave. Thus has been born the culture seen in America today.

What is little known by most people is that science, for centuries the thorn in the side of theism, has in the past fifty years become its pulpit. A series of recent discoveries, all accepted by the scientific community as evidential, has cast serious doubts on the atheist's case. For one thing, the presumption of an eternal universe seems to be inaccurate. Though admittedly billions of years old, it has been found (through the measurement of its *background radiation*) to have had a definite beginning in time. Once thought to be random, it seems more likely (in light of what scientists call the *anthropic principle)* to be highly structured and precise, down to the smallest details. What's more, the whole purpose of this fine-tuning of the universe, the end to which the universe seems to be pointing, say the scientists, appears to be the existence of human beings. At the same time, the veracity of several key concepts of Darwinism has been called into question by the scientific community. The picture that science now gives us of the universe is that of a huge, precise, non-random, finite mechanism built for one purpose: human existence. It is as if science has found the hidden key, reopened the door, and brought us all face-to-face with the reality of God.[1]

the **Argument from Personal Testimony**

Day 52... the majority opinion

Day 53... conflicting testimony: whom do I believe?

Day 54... the author's testimony

Day 55... the universe's testimony
(the 5 arguments summarized)

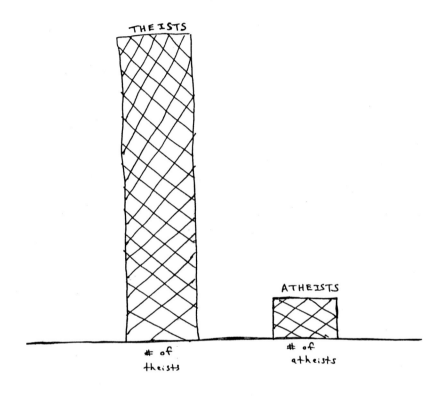

Figure 52:

Theists – A Vocal Majority

Atheists – A Vocal Minority

Day 52
the majority opinion

"According to various Gallup surveys, 94% of Americans believe in God and 90% pray."

- scientist PATRICK GLYNN

The last reason that I will offer for belief in God lies squarely in the realm of the subjective. I call this the *Argument from Personal Testimony*, because it directs our attention to the personal testimony of human beings throughout the ages concerning the reality of God and His effect on their lives.

In every time and culture, the notion that God exists has been the overwhelming consensus. You will not find one era where theism is overshadowed, one period where atheism reigns supreme. Sometimes that belief has been rather primitive and other times mature, but it has always been there, this tidal wave of opinion in the direction of God. He may be perceived by some cultures to be unapproachable and by others to be very near, but only occasionally has He been declared to be nonexistent. The theist, therefore, is solidly in the ranks of the majority, and there are no signs of any change on the horizon. If the weight of personal testimony is used as a gauge, to believe in God becomes the easy choice.

The majority is not always correct, however, and atheists are quick to point this out. The sad history of Copernicus and Galileo is evidence enough that strength in numbers is not always proportional to degree of truth. They alone were perceptive and brave enough to declare to an incredulous public that the earth was not the astronomical center of the universe. They, too, were in the minority, but they were on the side of right. Those in the majority were wrong, and they proceeded to compound their error by persecuting anyone whose opinions differed from their own. "It just might be the case," the atheists warn us, "that our minority opinion about God is also correct and will be proven so in due time."

This argument notwithstanding, I believe there is good reason to maintain, when it comes to belief in God, that the majority opinion is true. If it were not, I do not believe that theism would ever have remained the consensus opinion. Is it not amazing, once humanity conceded that Copernicus and Galileo were right, that belief in God went unscathed? Wouldn't it seem likely that theism would suffer when the fallacy of an earth-centered universe was exposed? How was it possible for such belief to remain supreme in the face of evidence that seemed to threaten it at its very core? I do not think it would have ever weathered that storm unless it was true.

Over the past two centuries, the continued embrace of theism by human beings in the face of the Scientific Revolution is likewise a paradox that can best be explained by its veracity. With the immense popularity of Darwin and Freud in the classroom and the neglect therein of creationism and traditional ethics, one would have expected atheism to have made huge gains. Within certain isolated populations, it did. By the year 2000, for example, 90% of psychologists had dismissed the existence of God as untrue, indeterminate, or irrelevant. These skeptics, however, still remain the overwhelming minority. The overall picture of humanity given to us by independent pollsters is of a group of people whose faith in God has refused to yield to cultural and scientific trends. Incredibly, ninety-four of every one hundred Americans still profess belief in God, a fact atheists would like to blame on the public's ignorance of any alternatives. I would assert that the ubiquity of humanism in public schools and college campuses over the past forty years makes it doubtful the masses believe in God simply because they are uninformed. The truth is they are well informed yet continue to believe.

Science and knowledge will continue to evolve. Old ideas will be discarded and new ones embraced. Discoveries will come that seem to undermine faith. Faith will not be phased. It will emerge stronger, wiser, and deeper. Belief in God will always remain the constant in the equation of the universe. It will never die, because truth never dies.

Figure 53:
The Verdict Is In

Day 53
conflicting testimony: whom do I believe?

"Christian theism must be rejected ... "

- atheist GEORGE H. SMITH

"The evidence of God's existence...is more than compelling..."

- philosopher BLAISE PASCAL

I have always been a little wary of making decisions based on subjective personal testimony. It can be very difficult to gauge the truth of what the person is saying, and I suspect that he or she may be inclined to spin the testimony in the most favorable light possible. What results is a witness that is a hybrid of that person's experience and perspective. It cannot really be trusted, for the same reason a personal testimony on a television infomercial can't be trusted: there may be a tendency to make things appear better or more certain than they are.

In such cases, I try to look for certain things that tend to lend credibility to the story. Does the person have anything to gain from it? If not, it is more likely to be true. Does he or she back up the story with objective evidence? If so, it is to be taken more seriously. Is the person, by giving the testimony, placed in a position where he or she may be criticized and penalized instead of praised and rewarded? If so, the testimony has much more the ring of truth to it. Is his or her testimony as a whole logical? If it is, it may merit a closer look.

I have already alluded to the fact that a good many atheists have changed their position and have begun to bear witness to the reality of God. I have recognized others who have made the change in the opposite direction, ex-theists who now espouse atheism. As I have sifted through their conflicting testimonies, admittedly through the lens of my own theism, I have noticed several things that make the converts to theism more believable.

If you analyze the collective witness of theists-turned-atheists, you will encounter one of five reasons for not believing in God. One is that scientific evidence points them toward atheism. The classic example is Darwin, who left on his famous excursion a Christian and returned an agnostic. Others point to all of the unjustified pain and suffering on earth as evidence that God doesn't exist. Charles Templeton, a former teammate of Billy Graham and the author of *Farewell to God: My Reasons for Rejecting the Christian Faith*, uses this approach. A third reason given is the inability of theists to prove beyond a doubt the existence of God. A fourth is the fact that theism has always been embraced by some who have acted in ways completely antithetical to its tenets. If theists answer these four accusations, all that remains for atheists to point to is their subjective intuition that atheism is right. Those who have already made up their minds usually make this final defense.

The collective witness of atheists-turned-theists is qualitatively different. Staunch atheists–men of intellect and leadership such as C. S. Lewis, Patrick Glynn, Lee Strobel, and Charles Colson–have begun to believe in God and have methodically defended their change of direction. Having been there before, they have exposed the following weaknesses in atheistic rhetoric:

1. when atheists use science as proof, they fail to acknowledge a whole body of scientific evidence that points *toward* God;
2. when they refer to the world's pain as evidence against God's existence, they fail to see that it's God's nature (not His existence) that is put on trial by suffering;
3. when they accuse theists of being unable to prove their case, they are the proverbial "pot calling the kettle black;"
4. when they point to religion's atrocities as reason to abandon faith, they fail to acknowledge that the good done in the name of God far outweighs the bad, that democracy has its warts as well and they

have yet to abandon it;

5. when they refuse to change their position no matter the argument, all they are left with as the basis of their belief is subjective opinion—hearsay and hunch—with little or no objective foundation.

Contrast this with the converts to theism above, who use rational arguments to buttress their subjective beliefs, rational arguments that have stood the test of time. Their personal testimony rests squarely upon an objective foundation. For this reason, their witness seems to me the most credible, the kind most likely to sway an impartial jury.

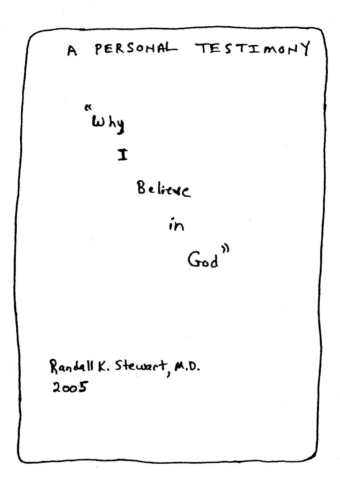

Figure 54:

Objectivity + Subjectivity

Day 54
the author's testimony

"Increase our faith!"

- the DISCIPLES of Jesus

"I believe; help my unbelief!"

- a FATHER who brought his sick son to Jesus

In the introduction to this book, I gave you a bit of my own personal testimony. I told you about my early belief in the existence of God, a belief that was more a product of my upbringing than anything else. Unaware of any evidence to the contrary, I accepted as true virtually everything I heard about God at home and church. In college, however, I encountered a skepticism about God that totally went against the grain of my youth. There I studied the greatest philosophers who ever lived and soon discovered that some of them were avowed atheists.[1] As much as I would have liked, I could not easily discard their passionate and persuasive arguments. Just as troubling was the fact that I had no answers to give them. I was a novice in the area of theology and philosophy and, in every sense of the phrase, was in water way over my head. Inevitably, my rock-solid faith began to show some cracks. I began to doubt.

Thus began for me a religious journey that continues to the present, a journey of persistent faith in the midst of lingering doubt. Through the years, I sought and found satisfactory answers to the rhetoric of atheists and agnostics. Forced daily in my role as a physician to weigh diagnostic and therapeutic evidence in the balance, I found it rather easy to analyze the arguments for and against God and discard the ones that were marginal. The others I put under a microscope with three lenses: the lens of reason, the lens of common sense, and the lens of practicality. Only those arguments that were all three–rational, sensible, and livable–were embraced by me as true.

After years of such study and reflection, I have come to the conclusion that my childhood faith in God was legitimate, that it could withstand all of the doubts and uncertainties put in its way. The existence of God, a belief I took for granted in my youth and thoroughly dissected as a young adult, is now to me a proven hypothesis that has been tried and tested in the "laboratory" of my mind, emotions, and experience. While I cannot truthfully claim to have eliminated every parcel of doubt, I can claim that my life today as a theist–in the midst of some occasional doubts–is more rewarding, meaningful, challenging, and fulfilling than ever before.

In a sense, I left the simple faith of my youth to seek the path of truth, only in the end to find myself back where I started. Although I still, like Paul,[2] see the world through a lens that is not completely transparent, the prism of my faith is clear enough to see in the landscape of the universe the face of God. In the knowledge of His presence, I have found peace.

the "Argument from Design"
|
the "Argument from Fairness"
|
the "Argument from Supernatural Belief"
|
the "Argument from Human Characteristics"
|
the "Argument from Personal Testimony"

Figure 55:
Five Reasons to Believe in God

Day 55
The universe's testimony (the 5 arguments summarized)

"Nothing in this world is able to explain its own existence; thus, there must be a God in order to explain the world in which we find ourselves."

- apologist JOHN WARWICK MONTGOMERY

If I was given five minutes to tell you why you should believe in the existence of God, I would relate to you what has made sense in my own experience. First of all, I would limit our discussion to these two possibilities: theism ("He exists!") and atheism ("He does not!"). In so doing, I would eliminate agnosticism ("I'm not sure!") as a viable option, simply because it cannot be true. If we knew all the facts about the existence of God, agnosticism would become extinct, leaving theism or atheism—whichever is true—as the only logical choice.

Next, I would admit to you that any argument for or against God's existence will fall short of absolute proof. Nevertheless, I would assert that it is imperative for you to make a decision one way or the other based on the evidence at hand, for only at work in one of the "fields" (theism or atheism) can anything meaningful be accomplished.

After this brief introduction, I would share with you five arguments for God's existence:

1. the **Argument from Design** - *Everyone in the world is aware that there is order and design in the universe. Just as the presence of design in a watch demands the existence of a watchmaker, the presence of design in the universe demands the existence of a Creator. To deny this, you must assert, in the face of scientific evidence to the contrary, that the universe is eternal and in no need of a Creator. Or you must claim, contrary to common sense, that the universe is an illusion and in no need of a Creator. You, of course, could point to all the disorder in the world as evidence against God,*

but that is evidence concerning God's character. It has nothing to do with whether or not He exists.

2. *the* **Argument from Fairness** - *Everyone has a sense that some things in life are unfair. It follows, therefore, that something called "fairness" must also exist. This standard of fairness–this belief that some things are right and others are wrong, this Moral Law within us–could not have come from nature or from humans, because rules must always transcend the "playing field" and the "players." The existence of this Moral Law within us demands the existence of God. You could, like atheists, try to deny this by saying that there is no such thing as fair/unfair or right/wrong if the universe is 100% the product of chance. The next moment, however, you will proceed to act as if you are right and I am wrong. You will find yourself unable to live what you preach.*

3. *the* **Argument from Supernatural Belief** - *As far back as history can be recorded, human beings have believed that something other than nature exists. This awareness of a supernatural world could not have entered their minds without God's help any more than awareness of the world of William Shakespeare could enter the minds of Romeo and Juliet without Shakespeare's help. The existence of supernatural belief, therefore, demands the existence of the supernatural. Without God's assistance, no one could have ever conceived that He was possible. You may, like atheists, try to deny this by claiming supernatural belief to be a by-product of nature, but what you are claiming does not make sense. If nature is all there is, as atheists assert, it would be an extreme contradiction to claim that it could relate to humans a belief in the existence of something outside itself. The conclusion is: God must be the source of our supernatural awareness.*

4. *the* **Argument from Human Characteristics** - *To be consistent with the principle of cause and effect, you must believe your human*

traits to have originated from a source consistent with them. Just as apples must come from apple trees, your reason and your sense of morality and purpose must come from a source that is rational, moral, and purposeful. Atheists may claim nature to be that source, but their view of nature—100% irrational, 100% amoral, and 100% without purpose—makes the effect unexplained by its cause. Or they may claim, as many atheists do, that human characteristics like morality and purpose do not really exist. The problem is that they proceed to act in their daily lives as if they do. Then they try to point to our negative traits as evidence against God, but this is just an attempt to change the subject. They know that their view of nature can explain why humans are sometimes irrational, immoral, and purposeless. But the question at hand is whether or not the atheists' worldview can account for the many times humans are rational, moral, and purposeful. The answer is: it cannot. You must conclude, therefore, that the presence of such human characteristics in us demands the existence of a source with similar characteristics. It demands the existence of God.

5. *the* **Argument from Personal Testimony** *- Belief in God has been the consensus testimony throughout history, even during the rise of cultural and scientific trends that have tended to undermine its credibility. The "roll call" of such theists today includes many former atheists who have embraced the existence of God as the most sensible explanation for what they know about the universe and what they experience in it. My personal testimony is the same. Although never an atheist, I have through the years had some doubts about God, only to see the vast majority of them vanish in the spotlight of truth.*

These are my reasons for believing in God. The first four form an objective foundation upon which the fifth rests. They are an integral part of my faith. My hope is that they will be of some benefit to yours.

Closing Steps

Day 56… what about the Bible?

Day 57… friends of other faiths

Day 58… common sense

Day 59… many maps, one treasure

Day 60… the summit of God's existence

Figure 56:

Quoting Scripture to the Atheist –
A Waste of Time

Day 56
what about the Bible?

"Mr. Crampton, I don't believe that [Bible] story ..."

- a young STUDENT, to his Sunday School teacher

We need to tie up a few loose ends before we conclude. First of all, I want to make you aware that thus far the Bible has seldom been referred to on our journey. Its few citations have been restricted to quotations relevant to the argument at hand and to general truths which both theists and atheists would accept. You may have already noticed this dearth of scripture and may have assumed such an omission to be an accident. It was not. In fact, it was by design. You have seen few Biblical references along the way because that was what I intended from the start. At first, this may seem to theists a bit hypocritical. Why would I, a professing Christian who loves and reveres the Bible, not include it herein? If I consider it to be true, why would I ignore it? If I am arguing about the existence of God, how could I omit a source so pivotal to that belief, one whose first four words are, "In the beginning, God..."?

The reason I have refused to use it is rather simple. What I have tried to do is give everyone journeying with us some valid reasons for believing in God. I have assumed that theists have been the majority in our travel group. They have chosen to come along because the subject has peaked their curiosity, perhaps because they have sensed a desire to buttress their beliefs. Several in our party, however, have been atheists, and this has presented me with a problem when it comes to the Bible. Atheists, you see, do not believe that the Bible is true. They do not consider it to be credible testimony any more than I would consider the testimony of a hostile witness credible. I would have been, at best, accused by them of circular reasoning if I had argued, "I believe in God, because the Bible says God exists." They probably would have responded with something like this: "I don't believe in God, because my mind tells me God doesn't exist." Given the choice between the witness of the Bible and the witness of their own intellect, they would quickly embrace the latter and discard the former. In short, the Bible is to the atheist an unreliable source. It would be considered by him to be biased testimony, the kind you would expect a good jury to mistrust.

What I have chosen to do as your guide is to start at a point where we all can agree and proceed from there. I have tried over the past eight weeks to lead all of my readers, both theists and atheists, on a path toward belief in God that has taken into account the presuppositions they have brought with them. I have attempted to start at the common ground of theists and atheists instead of embarking from their areas of contention. Purposely avoiding calling the Bible to the stand in God's defense, I have chosen instead to submit as evidence the universe which all of us encounter every day. What do we know and perceive about the universe around us, and how can it best be explained? Does the kind of world we live in make the most sense with or without a God behind it? Is our human make-up more likely the product of nature or the supernatural? Is it more rational, given our knowledge of ourselves and the universe, to believe in God or deny His existence? This has been the type of argument I have put before you from the first day until now. In doing so, I have chosen a path that has steered us clear of Bible verses as proof texts.

Be assured that this detour is only temporary. At a later leg of our journey, after we have tackled the existence of God and the natures of both God and man, I will lead you on a path lit with such verses. I will at that time use the Bible freely, holding it high before you in public with the same zeal that, even now, I feel for it in my heart. Until then, the theist should be comforted (and, I think, the atheist troubled) that a strong case can be made for God's existence even with the Bible temporarily placed on the shelf. If anything, this will make us respect the Bible all the more when, in due time, we pick it up again.

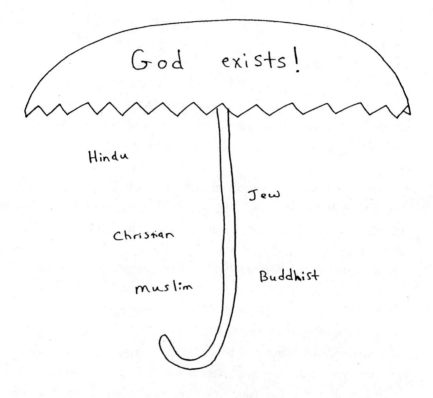

Figure 57:
The Broad Umbrella of Theism

Day 57
friends of other faiths

"We have not yet got as far as the God of any actual religion, still less the God of that particular religion called Christianity."

- apologist C. S. LEWIS

I also want to make you aware that no evidence has yet been offered that would tend to favor one religion over another. Jews, Hindus, Buddhists, Muslims, and Christians should agree with the main point of this book. They may use different sources for their quotations and approach the argument from different angles, but they would all come to the same conclusion about the existence of God. They all would claim that a God or, in some cases, a group of several gods exists. Pertaining to the subject at hand, they are on the same side of the fence. They all are theists. They are working in the same "field."

On another leg of our journey, we will compare the major religions and see if there is one that is preferable. As a follower of Jesus, you can correctly assume that I will propose Christianity to be the standard-bearer of the truth. I will do so, hopefully, with a sense of respect for the adherents of other faiths and with an understanding and tolerance of them that, in my opinion, is sorely lacking in society today. Regarding the present issue, that of the existence of God, they are my friends. As fellow theists, we walk side by side as the first leg of our journey draws to a close.

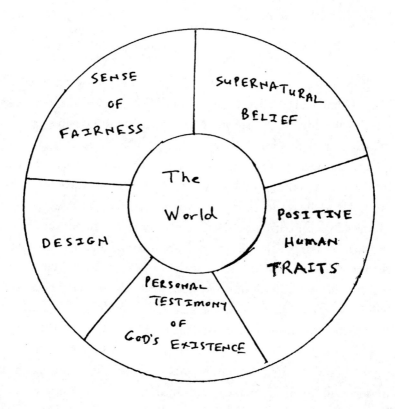

Figure 58:

The Wheel of Common Sense

Day 58
common sense

"... faith is not an irrational leap...[It is] supported by reason and evidence."

- Christian apologist CHARLES COLSON

Throughout this journey, we have tried to approach the existence of God from a commonsense standpoint. Instead of blindly, even stubbornly, believing in God, we have attempted to discover if there are any objective reasons for theistic faith. As we have taken this look at the world around us, we found five things that we *know* are true, five observations about our universe that we *all* can agree are factual. These five are as follows:

1. Humans live in a universe that shows evidence of order and design.
2. Humans tend to have a notion that some things are fair/unfair and right/wrong.
3. Humans have throughout history believed in the existence of the supernatural.
4. Humans everywhere possess certain characteristics considered to be positive.
5. Humans abound who will gladly give personal testimony of God's existence.

After stating these concrete truths, we have attempted to find the best explanation for them:

1. Are the order and design in the universe best explained by God or without Him?
2. Is our sense of fairness/unfairness and right/wrong more reasonable in a theistic or an atheistic universe?

3. Is humanity's tendency toward supernatural belief best accounted for by a universe governed by God or a universe governed by nature?
4. Are our positive human characteristics more likely the product of a world that is 100% natural or one that includes the supernatural?
5. Does the consensus testimony of individuals in all ages of God's existence make the most sense to us if that testimony is true or if it is false?

These are the five facts we have observed and the five questions we have raised about them. In the final analysis, there has been but one answer: the existence of God is the best explanation. Belief in God, it turns out, has had much more the ring of truth to it than atheism. When put to the test, theism has earned the seal-of-approval of our common sense.

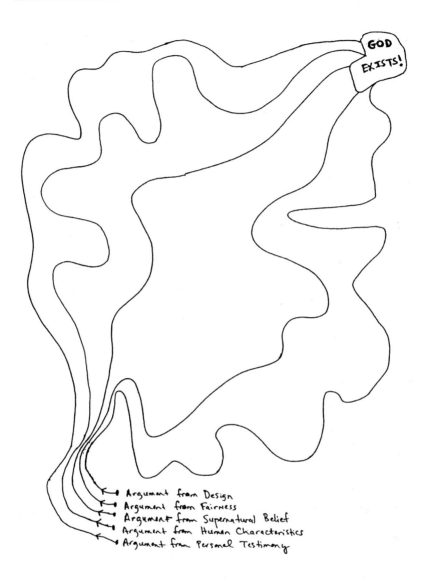

Figure 59:

5 Paths to the
Same Treasure

Day 59
many maps, one treasure

"...atheism cannot credibly account for...the
fine-tuning of the universe,...the existence of
moral laws, the supernatural confirmation..."

- investigative reporter LEE STROBEL

As we have progressed through my five reasons for believing in God, I suspect that one or two of them may have resonated with you more than the others. This is to be expected, given the varied backgrounds, knowledge, and experience among us. Unfortunately, the tendency sometimes is for the religious seeker to become concerned if he or she cannot embrace all of these arguments. I want to correct this misunderstanding once and for all. What the reader must realize is that the numerous arguments for God's existence (one writer has listed two dozen of them) are not like a series of sums leading to one right answer. They are not linked in sequence so that one bad one ruins the whole equation. They are more like separate maps to the same treasure; if only one of them is right, then the treasure exists.

In a sense, I have given you five maps to the treasure of God's existence. Some of them for various reasons may have led you to a dead end. You may have had to turn back and try the other ones. But if any one has led you to the treasure, it matters not if the others failed you. You have sought and found the reality of God. Instead of worrying about the maps that did not work, a time for celebrating the one that did would seem the proper course. My advice to you, then, is to become acquainted with the five arguments given in this book and others alluded to elsewhere, latch on to one or two that ring true with you, ride these to your destination, and quit worrying that you have left the other arguments behind.

Figure 60:

The First Leg of Our Journey Comes to an End

Day 60
the summit of God's existence

> *"For the scientist who has lived by his faith in the power
> of reason, the story ends like a bad dream. He has scaled
> the mountains of ignorance; he is about to conquer the
> highest peak; as he pulls himself over the final rock, he is
> greeted by a band of theologians who have been sitting
> there for centuries."*

- astronomer and NASA director ROBERT JASTROW

In his letter to the church at Rome, the apostle Paul argued that humans should be able to come to believe in God just by looking at the world around them. Even if no family was there to tell them, if no angel was sent to enlighten them, if no Bible was there to inspire them, they could perceive "God's invisible qualities—his eternal power and divine nature"—by looking at "the things that are made." I have come to the conclusion that Paul was right. You and I are no different in many ways than primitive man and woman millions of years ago. We may not be as illiterate and superstitious as they were, but we inhabit the same universe, a universe that bears the handprint of God. God first planted the seed of His awareness in us, then put us in a universe with evidence of Himself all around us. If we would just take the time to look at the world in which we live and take the effort to consider from whence it came, that seed would begin to take root, sprout, and bloom.

That is exactly what many of you have tried to do on this journey. Over the past sixty days, you have invested much time and effort trying to cultivate that seed. My prayer is that the same God who planted that seed in you will reward you with a harvest, that you may come to trust and believe and receive the reality of God in your life.

With this "amen," we have reached the end of the first leg of our journey. Perhaps I will meet you again at a later stage of your pilgrimage. Until then, be assured that I will always be grateful for the opportunity to have ascended the slope of God's existence with you. My faith in God has grown even stronger as together we have walked over territory that is now very familiar to me. I encourage you, if stronger faith you likewise desire, to retread these same steps in the near future. Whether you use the printed word or the illustrations, or both, in your subsequent climbs, the results should be the same. You should with each trip better understand and more tightly embrace the reality of God. In this case, familiarity will breed contempt's opposite: reverence.

AFTERWORD

The subject of God's existence has never generated a shortage of passion and opinion. It has always had the potential to be controversial and to become a nidus of polarization. The book you have just read is no exception. It will, I predict, foster criticism from several sources. Unless persuaded otherwise as they read, atheists will disagree entirely with its conclusion and will try to poke holes in its arguments. Most agnostics will do the same and will remain skeptical and unconvinced. Ironically, the strongest reservations will most likely be voiced by fellow theists, people who share with me a belief in God but object to my approach, emphasis, or style. Some of them will say that my arguments have been too objective. Others will find them too subjective. Some will say that I have described God in terms much too personal, and as a result the awe and mystery of divine transcendence have been ignored. Many will counter with just the opposite, that the book has not emphasized God's personality enough, making Him so distant that He seems irrelevant to everyday life. Some will assert that the entire book is a waste of time and mental effort, since God's existence should be assumed and not argued, reverenced and not rationalized. Some will consider my approach much too Christian, while others will be disappointed that it is not Christian enough. Some will opine that I have led them on a path much too laden with clever analogies and simplistic illustrations, while a few will probably accuse me of talking "over their heads." When all is said and done, negative reaction to what I have written will range from boredom to disappointment to disgust.

I am not surprised nor upset by these criticisms. In fact, I understand and accept them. I believe that each of them exposes a potential weakness in the way I have chosen to deal with the subject of God. The reason I have decided to proceed, even with full knowledge of these limitations and liabilities, is that I firmly believe a subset of theists exists who will find this book beneficial. I am convinced that there are many people today professing a belief in God who, just as I did for several years, are struggling with His existence. The number of such people is more than it appears at first glance, because I am certain that the majority conceals these doubts from family and peers, relegating them to moments of quiet introspection. Their crisis of faith, I believe, is very similar to what I experienced and its solution, I hope, the same. If any of these individuals reads what I have written, relates it to his or her religious journey, and finds it a useful adjunct to his or her faith, then the book will have achieved its intended purpose.

As we shall see in the next leg of our journey, the way theists have dealt with the reality of God has varied considerably from person to person and from time to time. Indeed, the way He is perceived by each individual tends to evolve and change over the course of a lifetime. I am no different. Even today, I sometimes perceive God to be transcendent, distant, Wholly Other. At other times, I sense Him immanent, relational, and personal. Often my faith is objective and rational but just as often subjective and mystical. As I will later explain, I have adopted a faith that can be described as a balance of these opposites, a faith that embraces a God who is paradoxically both transcendent and personal, a faith that approaches Him with a blend of reason and mystery.

If this book has not seemed to reflect this dynamic balance in my faith, I hope the reader will understand why. The arguments atheists used years ago to create doubt within me about God's existence were largely objective ones. It was natural that my path back from doubt to faith would likewise be objectively bent. For this reason, I fear that this book does not tend to give the subjective dimension of my faith its due. This is, at least, the feeling that I get every time I have read it in its entirety. If you, too, have sensed this apparent imbalance, then trust me that it has been a temporary, albeit necessary, distortion. Now that I have revealed to you how I came to fully believe in God again, I feel no compulsion to handle the subject of God's nature the same way. I will certainly approach this next topic objectively and rationally, but I predict that this time you will be able to better appreciate the subjective and mysterious side of my faith.

Toward the completion of this book, I fortuitously reread Karen Armstrong's *A History of God*, in which she provides "a history of the way men and women have perceived him from Abraham to the present day." She is able to capture better than anyone I have read the tension that has existed throughout history between God's transcendence and His immanence, between a faith in Him that is subjective versus one that is objective. Her work once again showed me that humans have always seemed to wrestle with the balance of reason and mystery in religion. Instead of trying to eliminate or avoid this paradox, my own view is that we all should seek to embrace it, accepting it as an integral part of the religious experience. I believe that God is both transcendent and personal and can be experienced both objectively and subjectively. I include both reason and mystery in my faith. My faith, in fact, consists of holding these opposites within me in permanent, dynamic tension.

We will discuss this in more detail when we begin to examine God's nature. As we do so, the question of His existence should not trouble us any longer. It will be assumed, based on the testimony given in this book, that God exists and that humanity's inclination toward faith in Him has not been in vain. We will accept faith in God as something indigenous to men and women.

In the introduction to her book, as she recounts her own religious journey from life as a nun to that of a religious skeptic, Ms. Armstrong agrees that we are all in the same boat:

> ...my study of the history of religion has revealed that human beings are spiritual animals. Indeed, there is a case for arguing that *Homo sapiens* is also *Homo religiosus*. Men and women started to worship gods as soon as they became recognizably human; they created religions at the same time as they created works of art. This was not simply because they wanted to propitiate powerful

forces; these early faiths expressed the wonder and mystery that seem always to have been an essential component of the human experience of this beautiful yet terrifying world. Like art, religion has been an attempt to find meaning and value in life, despite the suffering that flesh is heir to. Like any other human activity, religion can be abused, but it seems to have been something we have always done. It was...natural to humanity... I expected to find that God had simply been a projection of human needs and desires... I have been extremely surprised by some of my findings.

So have I been pleasantly surprised about the reality of God. I have found that He is not a product of my fears and wishes, nor is He merely an extension of the forces of nature all around me. I have discovered that God truly exists and that His existence would not change if I (and all my needs and fears) and nature (and all its beauty and fury) were to pass away. That realization has made all the difference in my life.

ENDNOTES

Day 1

[1]When I say that it would be foolish to proceed forward if God does not exist, I am not implying that one's mind must be completely made up about God's existence before the subject of His nature can be considered. I am aware of several people, now professing and practicing theists, who looked at these two aspects of God simultaneously as they made their decision. While remaining unconvinced that God was real, they tried to imagine what He would be like if He was. I see no problem with this approach, except that it can incline the seeker to get ahead of himself and lead to appropriate questions being asked at inappropriate times, often with disastrous consequences. (Take, for example, the temptation to use the presence of evil and suffering in the world—a discussion relevant to God's nature—as a reason to deny His existence.) If the seeker can keep his or her mind clear that the subjects of God's existence and nature are two separate legs of the same journey and can remain aware of the differences inherent therein, then to proceed along these dual fronts should not be discouraged. I do, however, think it ludicrous to go any further when one has already made up his or her mind that there is no God. And if it were ever proven that he or she is right, then it would be foolish for any of us to continue. It would be a waste of anyone's time to try to figure out the nature of a nonexistent God.

Day 2

[1]In my own Protestant denomination, there are many who claim that Christianity is not a religion. It is, instead, a relationship. It is not man seeking God, but God seeking man. While I agree that there are some significant qualitative differences in the way Christians and other theists perceive their interaction with God and am convinced of the benefits a personal relationship with Jesus brings to the individual, the way I broadly define religion allows me to include Christianity along with all the other faiths. Very simply, if you belong to a group that worships God or the gods, you belong to a religion. That is as far as my definition goes.

Day 3

[1]For a review of the scientific evidence in favor of an afterlife, read "Intimations of Immortality" in Patrick Glynn's *God: The Evidence* (Roseville, Calif.: Prima Publishing, 1999).

Day 4

[1]Psalm 10:1-15; 94:3-7.
[2]Job 13:3; 23:1-7.
[3]Matthew 27:46.
[4]Although atheism asks its adherents to deny ultimate justice in the world, the truth is that no atheist acts as if this is so. The *Argument from Fairness* (Days 32-34) will elaborate further on this inconsistency.

Day 6

[1]When referring to God, I have chosen throughout this book to use the traditional masculine pronoun. I am aware of the debate about such use in certain theological and political circles and am not trying to be insensitive to those with differing views. If the truth were known, I believe that God, neither male nor female, transcends the bounds of gender just as much as the Divine transcends the bounds of race. Why I have elected to use "He," "His," and "Him" exclusively is rather practical. If theology isn't already confusing enough to the non-theologian, equally distributed references to God as masculine and feminine would have made this book much more difficult to follow. It would have defeated the purpose of the whole project: to relay God's existence to the masses in the most understandable terms possible. Another option—to refer to God as "It"—would have projected an image far too impersonal, almost demeaning. And to use no pronouns whatsoever would have made these pages unbearable reading.

Two other points are worth mentioning. Since most people are already accustomed to masculine references to God, their use here may help keep the reader focused on the main issue—is there a God?—rather than on a secondary one—whether God is male, female, or neuter. Lastly, and not the least important, Jesus freely used the male pronoun for God. I suspect he did so for similar practical reasons: to maximize the message and minimize the minutia. If such an approach was good enough for him, so be it for me.

Day 7

[1]Some would venture a third option, namely that God should not be thought of as either existing or not existing. It is futile, they would say, for us to try to define by these or any other terms what is utterly indescribable and transcendent. These mystics, as they are often called, shun any objective approach to God, relying entirely on subjective acknowledgement and worship. Such wholesale abandonment of the intellect has never satisfied me. On the other hand, to rely only on reason and totally dismiss mystery seems no better. My personal faith is actually a blend of the two, as tangible as the wind but just as elusive. For more on this, I refer you to this book's "Afterword."

Day 8

[1]In a very real sense, the atheist is less likely than the theist to approach certainty. He has the unenviable task of trying to prove a negative. His job is to prove that God is not, while the theist's is to prove that God is. The philosophers tell us that his task, for this very reason, is much more difficult. See "The Absurdity of Atheism" in Steve Kumar's *Christianity for Skeptics*.

Day 11

[1]Agnosticism, in fact, is so impractical that virtually every person I have read who espouses it is indistinguishable from an atheist. The agnostic Bertrand Russell is a classic example. He professes to be an agnostic, but his rhetoric and outlook are nothing short of atheistic. There is seldom a hint in his writings of the ambiguity he claims to possess about God. While maintaining that he spends his life straddling the fence, he speaks as one who has decided to work in the "field" of the atheists. I am sure there are some agnostics as well inside the church who appear in every respect to be theists. You would never guess they are unsure about God, because they decided long ago to inhabit and embrace the theist's world. They, like all agnostics, have found it impossible to remain on the fence. The daily lives of agnostics, therefore, are witness enough to the fact that agnosticism is not livable.

Day 15

[1]Credit is usually given to William Paley, the nineteenth century philosopher, for the watch-watchmaker analogy used today to explain

the *Argument from Design*. My rendition here is based on a paraphrase of Paley in Bruce Barton's *What Can a Man Believe?*

Day 16

[1]The *Argument from Design* is, in reality, much older than two hundred years. Indeed, there are variations of it in Jewish and Islamic writings early in the second millennium. It was not until the eighteenth century Enlightenment that Christian philosophers, like Paley and Voltaire, began to restate it and others, like David Hume, sought to discredit it.

Day 19

[1]I am afraid that I will lose a few supporters here. Science's claim that the universe is finite comes with another–that its beginning took place billions of years ago. All creationists would applaud the former, but Biblical literalists would take offense with the latter. They contend that the earth is no more than a few thousand years old and have written at length in defense of that opinion. If you are among them, I ask that you overlook our disagreement on the universe's age in deference to our agreement on its finitude. If you think about it, the fact that the universe had a beginning is the more central of the two issues. Whether that birth took place thousands or billions of years ago pales in comparison. Peripheral also is whether God chose the Big Bang to bring the world into being or merely shouted it into existence *ex nihilo*. The core issue–"in the beginning, God created the heavens and the earth"–is upheld either way. So if you disagree with the scientists and me about these side issues, I implore you to continue on with the group. I will not ask you to change your opinion; it, indeed, may be right. When we get to heaven and know the whole truth, I may be the one whose opinion must change. What I do ask of you is to save this discussion for a later date. Now is the time to stand on common ground, not to wrestle in peripheral currents.

Day 21

[1]For a more detailed discussion of the Many Worlds Hypothesis, read Lee Strobel's *The Case for a Creator* (Grand Rapids: Zondervan, 2004), pp. 141-144.

[2]Strobel also includes an explanation of the Oscillating Model of the

Universe in the work just cited, pages 113-117.

Day 29
[1]For a thorough, easy-to-read, and entertaining discussion of this argument, read Paul Chamberlain's *Can We Be Good Without God?* (Downers Grove, Ill.: InterVarsity, 1996).

Day 36
[1]The bulk of this argument is a recounting of C. S. Lewis in *Mere Christianity* (New York: Macmillan, 1943), Book I.

Day 40
[1]One of the objections to this argument goes like this:

If humanity's awareness of the supernatural implies that the supernatural is real, then our similar beliefs in Santa Claus, the Tooth Fairy, ghosts and goblins, and the like would imply that they are real, too. And since we all know that they aren't real, the *Argument from Supernatural Belief* does not pass the test. If you cannot apply it across the board, you should not use it to defend the existence of God.

The atheist continues by posing to us a question:

Do we, as adults, really believe in Santa Claus, ghosts and goblins, and the Tooth Fairy? Of course, not! We line up at Christmas to see him, not because we believe but rather because our children and grandchildren do. We place a tooth under the pillow at bedtime only because our child has faith in her. We do not. And we speak of ghosts and goblins around the campfire to scare the uninformed. We, the informed, realize that no such beings exist. Can't the same be said for belief in God? Isn't God a concept that with time and knowledge we will likewise outgrow? All we need is to be properly educated, and our belief in God will fade as quickly as a real Santa does in a young, maturing mind.

This argument, in essence, claims that God is a product of our imagination and informs us that all things imagined are not real. What it fails to ask (because it has no good answer) is this: where did our imagination come from? If it came from nature (this is what atheists would tell us), then nature is deceiving us. When we are children, she is allowing us via our imaginations to believe in the existence of creatures that really do not exist. And if nature is this much a liar when we are young, why should we believe her years later when she tells us via our "mature" brains that all imagination is false? Couldn't she be playing a trick on us again? Nature—now, as then—could be deceiving us, and it would be impossible for us to know the truth. The atheist may claim that he knows, but in making this claim he may be falling right into nature's trap. He may be making a wrong guess. He may be playing the role of nature's fool! Thus, when the atheist argues that all of our imagination—including our belief in God—is false, he finds himself placing his trust in the same nature that earlier led him astray.

The theist sees it all differently. He knows that there is a difference between believing in the supernatural in general and believing in the specific imaginary creatures alluded to above. Belief in the supernatural in general, as we shall see in this argument, could not have come from nature. If specific parts of that belief—imaginary beings like Santa Claus, the Tooth Fairy, and those ghosts—are later found to be false, supernatural belief in general does not end. Curiously, humanity as a whole has never abandoned the conviction that something other than nature is "out there." Neither should you. And there is no reason to believe nature if she tells you any differently.

Day 43
[1]The idea for today's analogy once again comes from Lewis' *Mere Christianity*.

Day 44
[1]A paraphrase of Jesus' words to the Samaritan woman as recorded in John's Gospel, chapter four.

Day 47
[1]Credit here is given to Greg Boyd for his ideas on cause and effect in *Letters from a Skeptic* (Colorado Springs: Chariot Victor, 1994), pp. 50-52, 54-57.

Day 49
[1]See *Mere Christianity*, Book I.

Day 50
[1]Fearing imprisonment, Hume left unpublished his *Dialogues*

Concerning Natural Religions, in which he launched his counter-attack on the *Argument from Design* that is summarized in today's reading.

Day 51

[1]I am not a physicist. For this reason, I chose not to include in the main text a detailed account of how the dual discoveries of background radiation and the anthropic principle have seriously called into question the atheist's belief in a random and eternal universe. These concepts involve mathematical formulas far too technical for my level of training. If I were asked to explain the two discoveries in terms the average non-scientist could understand, I would (after making apologies to the physicists for over-simplification) use the following analogy:

> Suppose that you and I, while driving through a busy city, happen to notice the smoke and rubble of a multi-story building that has recently collapsed to the ground. At first, we assume that this collapse was purely random, the chance result of blind forces (wind, erosion, gravity, etc.) acting in concert. Upon closer inspection, however, we notice several peculiarities about the debris that make us question its randomness. For one thing, we see that the building has collapsed in such a way that no structure nearby is affected. In addition, a broken clock we find in the rubble shows that the time of the collapse was three in the morning, the exact time when traffic and pedestrians would be at a minimum. Furthermore, a quick glance at the site from a distance indicates that the building seems to have fallen symmetrically, as if a giant foot has caved it in from top to bottom.
>
> Our curiosity getting the best of us, we decide to study this site and determine what really happened. We enlist a corps of engineers to assist us in our efforts. They are able to analyze the smoke and dust that has yet to settle to the ground and project from them the approximate time of the explosion. Remarkably, the time they come up with is very close to that on the broken clock we discovered. Within the structure the engineers find evidence of tiny explosives spaced at intervals that seem to have guaranteed a symmetric collapse. It is further determined that for the collapse of the building to be so symmetric, the timing of the detonation of the various explosives had to be just right. In fact, the experts discover that if only one of these explosives failed to fire or only

one fired at the wrong time, there would have been no chance at all for a safe implosion. Incredible as it seems, if the timing was off to any degree in the first half-second of the explosion, the engineers predict that the damage to nearby buildings and to any people in the area would have been great.

After days of such analysis, the engineers come to the unanimous conclusion that the collapse of the building was not a random event at all, that it was a designed and planned event, that the goal from the start was to explode the building in such a way that the city's architecture and population would be preserved. In short, what they discover was that the collapse of the building was caused by a nonrandom explosion that was organized from the beginning for one purpose: the betterment of the city.

Now scientists have believed for many years–based on evidence that the universe is expanding–that a big explosion, commonly called the Big Bang, started the whole process. In a sense, when the scientists look at the universe, they find themselves gazing at the aftermath, the rubble, of a cosmic explosion. For many years, the evidence seemed to suggest that this explosion was random and that any design seen within it today was the result of multiple blind forces acting in concert over billions of years. Man's and woman's existence, it seemed, could be attributed solely to chance. Then the scientists discovered background radiation in the universe and determined it to be the "smoke" left over from the Big Bang. They were then able to analyze this radiation and determine mathematically the approximate time of the explosion. The universe, it began to appear, had a definite beginning in time. It was not, as the atheists had hoped, eternal.

If that was not disconcerting enough, the atheists had to be alarmed even more by the discovery in the early 1970's of the anthropic principle. While analyzing the "rubble" of the universe, scientists found multiple constants (four in all: gravity, electromagnetism, the strong force, and the weak force) that had to be precisely timed and arranged to make life possible. They also found that if any one of these constants were altered to any degree in the first nanosecond of the Big Bang, life would never have occurred. In short, what the scientists discovered was that the Big Bang, far from being the random event heralded by the atheists, seems to have been a designed, nonrandom explosion orchestrated from the beginning for one purpose: the formation of life.

The implications of all this to belief in God are tremendous, as Patrick Glynn explains:

> For hundreds of years science had been whittling away at the proposition that the universe was created or designed. Suddenly, scientists came upon a series of facts that seemed to point toward precisely such a conclusion–that the universe is the product of intelligence and aim, that in the absence of intelligent organization of a thousand details vast and small, we would not exist...Today, moreover, the physicists find themselves constantly looking over their shoulder at the theologians, who watch with intrigue as the scientists are forced to wrestle anew with an issue they thought they had put to rest a long time ago: God...The anthropic principle...does offer as strong an indication as science and reason alone could be expected to provide that God exists.
> -Patrick Glynn, God: The Evidence (Roseville, Calif.: Prima Publishing, 1999), 8-9, 40, 55.

Day 54

[1]I want to make it clear that the religion curriculum at the Christian college I attended was not, in my opinion, out-of-balance. Included therein were courses that cemented traditional beliefs as well as those that challenged them. The college professors who taught them remain to this day dear to my heart. It would be an insult to them, and the furthest thing from the truth, to imply that they wanted to confuse and disillusion students preparing for the ministry. They were educators *par excellence* and considered a broad introduction to religious issues a requisite to service.

It was I, not the university or its teachers, who was out-of-balance. I entered college with no previous exposure to beliefs outside the narrow spectrum of evangelical Christianity. Although I was aware that atheists somewhere existed, I knew nothing of their arguments, much less any answer to them. If you could fault my religion professors any, they may have underestimated the impact such ideas can have on unsuspecting students, even those from solid Christian backgrounds. At the same time, they may have overestimated our ability to comprehend and internalize the counter-arguments they offered and thus may not have spent enough time on them. If this was my experience in a Baptist college, I can only imagine the plight of students attending other institutions where no apology is made for a bias toward atheism. Little can one wonder why so many people today consider faith in God obsolete or irrelevant.

The solution, it seems to me, would be early (pre-college) exposure of adolescents to atheistic and agnostic rhetoric and concomitant instruction in the answer of theists to it. We need not fear that such knowledge will make it more likely for high school students to abandon their belief in God. We, in medicine, know that mentioning suicide to the depressed patient does not make an attempted suicide more likely. In fact, the opposite is true. It allows us to recognize and deal with the problem before it happens. In the same way, telling our youth about atheism, far from turning their hearts in its direction, will be a preemptive strike against over-zealous atheistic teaching in their college years. The burden of this early, broad theological education falls squarely on the shoulders of two organizations: the family and the church.

[2] First Corinthians 13:12

Day 55

[1]If you are not acquainted with theological jargon and have no desire to learn it, then ignore this note. The rest of you may proceed. I want to try to mesh the five arguments just summarized with the traditional vernacular of the nineteenth century, when it was common to label such arguments as teleological, ontological, cosmological, or moralistic. *Teleology* has its roots in the Greek word "telos," which means "goal." In the context of God's existence, it refers to evidence that there is a purpose or goal behind the universe. The *Argument from Design* is the prototype, for it points to a divine Organizer behind the universe's obvious organization. *Ontology* has to do with cause and effect. The arguments in this category begin with the assumption that anything with a beginning must have a cause. As the name implies, those who use *cosmology* to argue God's existence look at the cosmos for evidence. But instead of focusing on the design therein, they behold the universe's complexity and declare that it is impossible to attribute this to chance. The anthropic principle provides such cosmological affirmation, for it traces the complexity of the universe to the first nanosecond of the Big Bang and tells us that such fine-tuning could not be random. In contrast, the *moralistic* argument looks inside,

not outside, humanity and sees there an internal moral compass that must have God as its source.

With this as the background, let's try to place my five arguments into these categories. Obviously, the second (the *Argument from Fairness*) is moralistic. And with their emphasis on cause and effect, the third and fourth arguments (from *Supernatural Belief* and *Human Characteristics*) can be considered ontological. The *Argument from Design*, as I have presented it, is actually a hybrid. As mentioned above, it is first and foremost teleological in nature. But it does not have any "teeth" to it unless it is ontologically true. As was noted previously (Days 17-18), design proves nothing if the universe is eternal. Only if the universe is finite–and, therefore, subject to ontology's rule of cause and effect–would the *Argument from Design* point us toward an Intelligent Designer. In addition, the *Argument from Design* is part cosmology, for the complexity of the universe is at its very foundation. The last of the arguments given, the one from *Personal Testimony*, does not fit into any of the classifications above. I call it an *experiential* argument, for it is based on subjective experience. I don't think this is a nineteenth century term, but it is inserted here to make our grouping complete.

The most positive thing about this classification system is that you don't really need it. You do not have to be aware of it or understand it to argue God's existence. If it helps you sort things out in your mind, use it. If it tends to confuse or amuse you, forget you ever heard about it.

BIBLIOGRAPHY OF QUOTATIONS

Day 1

D. Elton Trueblood, *General Philosophy* (Grand Rapids: Baker, 1963), 209.

Day 2

Madalyn Murray O'Hair, *What on Earth is an Atheist?* (New York: Arno, 1972), 38.

Day 3

Steve Kumar, *Christianity for Skeptics* (Peabody, Mass.: Hendrickson, 2000), 61.

Day 4

Robert J. Dean, *How Can We Believe?* (Nashville: Broadman, 1978), 25.

Day 5

Jean-Paul Sartre, "Existentialism," *Existentialism and Human Emotions* (trans. Bernard Frechtman; New York: Philosophical Library, 1957), 22.

Day 6

Bertrand Russell, *A Free Man's Worship* (Portland, Me.: Thomas Mosher, 1927), 6-7.

Day 7

J. L. Mackie, *The Miracle of Theism* (Oxford: Clarendon, 1982), 1.

Day 8

Madeleine L'Engle, quoted in: Lynn Anderson, *If I Believe, Why Do I Have These Doubts?* (Minneapolis, Minn.: Bethany House, 1992), 60.

Day 9

Edward Sillem, *Ways of Thinking About God* (London: Darton, Longman, & Todd, 1961), 1.

Day 10

Bertrand Russell, *What I Believe* (New York: C. P. Dutton and Co., 1925), 13.

Day 11

William Lane Craig, *Reasonable Faith* (Wheaton: Crossway, 1984), 72.

Day 12

C. Stephen Evans, *The Quest for Faith: Pointers to God* (Leicaster: InterVarsity, 1986), 131.

Hebrews 11:1 KJV

Day 13

Time, April 7, 1980, 65.

Day 14

"David Hume to John Stewart," February 1754, *The Letters of David Hume* (ed. J. Y. T. Greig; Oxford: Clarendon, 1932), 1.187.

Day 15

Quoted in Steve Kumar, *Christianity for Skeptics*, 10.

Day 16

Quoted in Steve Kumar, *Christianity for Skeptics*, 10.

Day 17

Norman Geisler, *False Gods of Our Time* (Eugene, Ore.: Harvest House, 1985), 52.

Day 18

Antony G. N. Flew and Thomas B. Warren, *The Warren-Flew Debate* (Jonesboro, Ark.: National Christian, 1977), 241.

Day 19

Robert Gange, *Origins and Destiny* (Waco, Tex.: Word, 1986), 8.

Day 20

Patrick Glynn, *God: The Evidence* (Roseville, Calif.: Prima Publishing, 1999), 20.

Ibid., 53-54, 26.

Quoted by the Baptist Press in *Baptist and Reflector* (Brentwood: Tennessee Baptist Convention Executive Board, December 22, 2004), 2.

Ibid.

Day 21

Quoted in Lee Strobel, *The Case for Faith* (Grand Rapids: Zondervan, 2000), 79.

Day 22

Steve Kumar, *Christianity for Skeptics*, 15.

Norman L. Geisler, *The Roots of Evil* (Grand Rapids: Zondervan, 1978), 18.

Norman L. Geisler, *Philosophy of Religion* (Grand Rapids: Zondervan, 1974), 312.

René Descartes, *Meditations on First Philosophy*, trans. Donald A. Cress (Indianapolis: Hackett, 1979), 17.

Day 23

Psalm 19:1,2 NIV

Day 24

C. S. Lewis, *The Problem of Pain* (New York: Macmillan, 1962), 13-15.

Day 25
Gregory A. Boyd and Edward K. Boyd, *Letters from a Skeptic* (Colorado Springs: Chariot Victor, 1994), 32.

Day 26
Quoted in Lee Strobel, *The Case for Faith*, 29.

Day 27
Edward K. Boyd and Gregory A. Boyd, *Letters from a Skeptic*, 22.

Quoted in Leslie D. Weatherhead, *Why Do Men Suffer?* (New York: Abingdon, 1936), 72.

C. S. Lewis, *The Best of C. S. Lewis* (New York: Hafner, 1969), 429.

Quoted in Lee Strobel, *The Case for Faith*, 31.

D. E. Trueblood, *General Philosophy*, 226.

Day 28
Steve Kumar, *Christianity for Skeptics*, 44.

Day 29
Immanuel Kant, *Critique of Pure Reason* (trans. by N. K. Smith; New York: St. Martin's, 1965), 166.

Day 30
Steve Kumar, *Christianity for Skeptics*, 25.

Day 31
Paul Chamberlain, *Can We Be Good Without God?* (Downers Grove, Ill.: InterVarsity, 1996), 51-52.

Day 32
Paul Chamberlain, *Can We Be Good Without God?*, 48.

Day 33
C. S. Lewis, *Mere Christianity* (New York: Macmillan, 1943), 29-30.

Day 34
Richard Taylor, *Ethics, Faith, and Reason* (Englewood Cliffs, NJ.: Prentice Hall, 1985), 65.

Day 35
Romans 2:15 NIV

Day 36
"Wittgenstein's Lectures on Ethics," *Philosophical Review*, 1965, 47:7.

Day 37
David Hugh Freeman, *A Philosophical Study of Religion* (Nutley, NJ.: Craig, 1964), 78.

Day 38
C. S. Lewis, *The Problem of Pain*, 15.

Day 39
Gregory A. Boyd and Edward K. Boyd, *Letters from a Skeptic*, 56.

Day 40
Quoted in Lee Strobel, *The Case for Faith*, 108.

Day 41
C. S. Lewis, *The Problem of Pain*, 15.

Day 42
Quoted in Vernon C. Grounds, *The Reason for Our Hope* (Chicago: Moody, 1945), 18.

Day 43
Psalm 14:1 NIV

Day 44
Thomas Cahill, *The Gift of the Jews* (New York: Nan Talese, 1998), 85-86.

Day 45
Quoted in Lee Strobel, *The Case for Faith*, 84

Day 46
Gregory A. Boyd and Edward K. Boyd, *Letters from a Skeptic*, 56.

Ronald Hepburn, in Antony Flew and Alasdair, *New Essays in Philosophical Theory* (New York: Macmillan, n.d.), 140.

Ernest L. Freud, ed., *Letters of Sigmund Freud* (London: Hogarth, 1961), 432.

Day 47
Edward Sillem, *Ways of Thinking about God*, 182.

Day 48
J. P. Moreland and Kai Nelson, *Does God Exist?* (Nashville: Thomas Nelson, 1990), 35.

Day 49
Edward K. Boyd and Gregory A. Boyd, *Letters from a Skeptic*, 53.

Day 50
Jules A. Baisnee, ed., *Readings in Natural Theology* (Westminster, Md.: Newman, 1962), 149.

Day 51
Patrick Glynn, *God: The Evidence*, 48.

Day 52
Patrick Glynn, *God: The Evidence*, 171.

Day 53
George H. Smith, *Atheism: The Case Against God* (Amherst, N.Y.: Prometheus Books, 1989), 51.

Blaise Pascal, *Pensees No. 430* (trans. H. F. Stewart; New York: Random House), [n.d.], [n.p.].

Day 54
Luke 17:5 RSV

Mark 9:24 RSV

Day 55
John Warwick Montgomery, *How Do We Know There Is a God?* (Minneapolis: Bethany Fellowship, 1973), 9.

Day 56
Quoted in Fleming Rutledge, *Help My Unbelief* (Grand Rapids: William B. Eerdmans Publishing, 2000), 190.

Day 57
C. S. Lewis, *Mere Christianity*, 29.

Day 58
Charles Colson, *How Now Shall We Live?* (Wheaton, Ill.: Tyndale House, 1999), 31-32.

Day 59
Lee Strobel, *The Case for Faith*, 252-253.

Day 60
Quoted in *Los Angeles Times*, June 25, 1978, Part VI, 1, 6.

Romans 1:19-20 NIV

Afterword
Karen Armstrong, *A History of God* (New York: Ballantine Books, 1993), xx.

Ibid., xiv.

SUGGESTIONS FOR GROUP STUDY

Session One: Introduction

Session Two: First Steps (Days 1-12)

Session Three: the *Argument from Design* (Days 13-28)

Session Four: the *Argument from Fairness* (Days 29-37)

Session Five: the *Argument from Supernatural Belief* (Days 38-45)

Session Six: the *Argument from Human Characteristics* (Days 46-51)

Session Seven: the *Argument from Personal Testimony* (Days 52-55)

Session Eight: Closing Steps (Days 56-60)

Session Nine: Afterword

Session One: Introduction

Group Activity

Objective: To examine the process by which belief can turn to doubt

1. Write on a sheet of paper three reasons you believed in Santa Claus as a child
2. List three reasons why you began to doubt that belief.
3. List three words that describe how you felt during that period of doubt.
4. List three things you did to work through your doubts and come to a final conclusion.

Group Study

Objective: To examine the author's religious journey from belief to doubt to belief again

1. Read the introduction to this book.
2. Discuss your overall impression of the author's introductory testimony.

Group Questions

Objective: To examine the group's personal experiences with religious belief and doubt

1. How did you first come to know about and/or believe in God? How was your introduction to God's existence similar to or different from that of the author?
2. Why did the author of this book begin to have doubts about God? Have you or someone you know had similar doubts? If so, how and when did they begin?
3. What results did these doubts about God have on the author? Did your doubts or those of your acquaintances have the same impact?

4. In your opinion, should the author have been exposed to atheistic philosophy in college? Was it good or bad that he never was told about the atheistic viewpoint during his formative years? (See "Endnotes, Day 54" for the author's answer.)

5. The author largely hid his doubts from everyone around him. Why do you think he did this? Do you believe there are many people in the church today who conceal such doubts?

6. How was the author able to confidently believe in God once again? What advice would you give someone who came to you with such doubts?

7. What do you think the author would say if asked if his journey from doubt to faith was worth the time and effort? Evaluate yourself: "Where am I on my journey?" Then challenge yourself: "Am I willing to take the steps necessary to move ahead?"

8. The author feels it important to treat atheists with honesty, dignity, and respect. Why do you think he feels this way? How are atheists different from you, and in what ways are you and they alike?

9. How would you classify yourself: a sometimes-a-doubt believer, a never-a-doubt believer, a sometimes-a-doubt nonbeliever (an agnostic), or a never-a-doubt nonbeliever (an atheist)? Are you satisfied with your classification?

Group Homework
Objective: To encourage individual preparation for Session Two

1. Read "First Steps" (Days 1-12).
2. Write down any questions or comments as you read.
3. Answer the following questions:
    a. What is your definition of religion?
    b. What advantages does belief in God offer you?
    c. Do you think that it is practical to live as an agnostic?
    d. Is your faith mostly subjective or objective, or is it a mixture of the two?

<u>Session Two</u>: First Steps (Days 1-12)

<u>Group Questions</u>
Objective: To understand the importance of theism

1. What is the main point of Figure 1? Does this mean that you must make a final decision about God's existence before you can begin to consider His character? (See "Endnotes, Day 1" for the author's answer.)

2. Look at Figure 2. What is your definition of religion? Do you include atheism as a religion? Are you aware that some people do not consider Christianity a religion? Why do they make this claim? What is your opinion? (See "Endnotes, Day 2" for the author's response.)

3. Review Figures 3, 4, 5, and 6. What four advantages of theism does the author cite? Which two are his favorites? Which do you think is most important?

4. Look at Figure 7. What does the author mean when he says that agnosticism can't be true?

5. What is the main point of Figure 8? Based on this figure, how would you define faith?

<u>Group Activity</u>
Objective: To understand the impracticality of agnosticism

1. Distribute to each participant a slip of paper with one of the following three statements written on it:
   a. "I believe the Tooth Fairy exists."
   b. "I do not believe the Tooth Fairy exists."
   c. "I'm not sure whether or not the Tooth Fairy exists."
   Tell them not to let anyone know which statement is on their slip.

2. Inform the group that, based on the statements on the slips of paper, some of them believe, some do not believe, and some are not sure that a Tooth Fairy exists. Tell them that their assignment is to guess which members of the group are the ones who are not sure.

3. Place a pillow and a garbage can in front of the class. Ask the class to pretend that it is now bedtime and that the slip of paper in their hands is a tooth they have just lost. Instruct them to come to the front one by one and, based on the statement on their paper, either put their "tooth" under the pillow as if the Tooth Fairy exists or into the waste basket as if she does not. As each individual proceeds to the front to do so, the others are to try to figure out which are the undecided. (Of course, the ones with the "I'm not sure..." slips of paper will have to decide which one of the two places to place their paper.)

4. After the activity is over, have the undecided group members identify themselves. Then ask the following questions: "Was it difficult to identify the undecided members? Why? When bedtime came and it was time to rest their heads on their pillows, what were they forced to do?"

5. Ask the group to look at Figures 9, 10, and 11. Ask them, "What is the main point of these illustrations? What do these figures have to do with the group activity we just finished?"

6. Read (or tell the class to read) the illustration given on Day 10. Ask: "Do you think it makes sense from a practical standpoint to be an agnostic?" Then ask: "How many people do you know who truly practice agnosticism?" (Refer them to "Endnotes, Day 11" for the author's answer.)

Group Study
Objective: To understand the definition of faith

1. Read Hebrews 11:1. What does this tell you about faith?

2. Look at Figure 12. What is its main point? Do you think that most people are aware of the objective dimension of faith? If not, why? Before now, were you aware that there were objective arguments for God's existence? Do you think such arguments would be helpful to some people? Why or why not?

Group Homework

Objective: To encourage individual preparation for Session Three

1. Read "the *Argument from Design*" (Days 13-28).
2. Write down any questions or comments as you read.
3. Make a list of the following:
   a. Five evidences of design in the universe not listed in Figure 13 or Day 13's reading
   b. Four design-designer relationships not listed in Figure 14 or Day 14's reading
   c. Three ways atheists have tried to rebut the *Argument from Design*
   d. Two evidences of disorder in the universe not given in Figure 24 or Day 24's reading
   e. One more answer given by some atheists to the *Argument from Design* (Day 20)

Session Three: the *Argument from Design* (Days 13-28)

Group Activity

Objective: To examine the basic principles of the *Argument from Design*

1. Bring two containers of Play-Doh to the class and ask for two volunteers to come before the group and create something out of the dough. Give them three minutes to complete their projects.
2. Leave the two "art works" in front of the group and ask: "How would you critique these 'works of art'? Do they show evidence of design?"
3. Refer the group to Figures 13 and 14 and ask: "What other evidences of design in the universe can you think of? What other design-designer relationships can you name?"
4. Refer the group again to the Play-Doh figures, then ask: "Suppose you walked into the room today and saw these Play-Doh 'works of art' on the table. Would you conclude that they had a creator or that they did not? Why or why not?"
5. Read the explanation on Day 15 of the *Argument from Design*.
6. Have the group look at Figures 15 and 16. Then ask: "How many of you were aware of the *Argument from Design* before today? What effect does the argument have on you?"

Group Questions

Objective: To examine two rebuttals of atheists to the *Argument from Design*

1. Refer to Figures 17 and 18. What counter-attack of the atheist to the *Argument from Design* is depicted in these figures? According to Figure 19, why has this rebuttal from the atheist recently lost credibility?

2. Refer to Figure 20. Is it helpful to know that scientists like Patrick Glynn and philosophers like Antony Flew have switched to theism? Does anyone in the group know of former atheists who now believe in God? According to the author (in the last paragraph of Day 20), conversions like these do not prove that God exists? Why not? What does he say they do prove? Do you think that people today are aware of the scientific evidence that points toward God? Is such evidence a part of the science curriculum in public schools? If not, should it be included?

3. Do you understand the two theories of the universe cited in Figure 21? Could anyone in the group state these two in their own words? If true, how would these two theories help the atheist in his fight against the *Argument from Design*? According to the quotation given on Day 21, what is William Lane Craig's opinion of these and other such alternate theories of the universe?

4. What second rebuttal to the *Argument from Design* is given in Figure 22? What two weaknesses of this rebuttal does the author cite?

5. Look at Figure 23 and review what we've covered thus far. What two rebuttals to the *Argument from Design* have we studied?

Group Study

Objective: To examine the most common rebuttal of atheists to the *Argument from Design*

1. Look at Figure 24 and read the four quotes given on Day 27. Have you ever heard anyone give similar reasons for not believing in God? Has the presence of such disorder in the universe caused you to sometimes question God's existence?

2. Read the illustration given on Day 26. What is its main point? What effect does this illustration have on your faith in God's existence?

3. Look at Figures 25 and 27. What is the main point of the two? Had it ever occurred to you that pain and suffering are not relevant to God's existence?

4. Look at Figure 28. If we exclude pain and suffering as reasons to deny God's existence, what three choices remain for the atheist to consider?

Group Homework

Objective: To encourage individual preparation for Session Four

1. Read "the *Argument from Fairness*" (Days 29-37).
2. Write down any questions or comments as you read.
3. Make a list of the following:
   a. Three things that everyone would consider wrong, no matter the situation
   b. Three things that everyone would consider right, no matter the situation
   c. Three rules of football, baseball, or basketball and the penalties for breaking them

<u>Session Four</u>: the *Argument from Fairness* (Days 29-37)

<u>Group Activity</u>
Objective: To understand why atheists believe nothing to be fair/unfair or right/wrong

1. Before the session, number twenty small pieces of paper from one to twenty, fold them, and place them in a container.

2. Have two group members compete in a game against each other to see who can draw a higher number. The person who does so gets one point. The first person to accumulate three points wins.

3. After the game is finished, ask the group: "Was this a game of chance or of skill? Can the loser of this game complain that the game was unfair? Why not?"

4. Refer the class to Figure 33 and ask: "What does this figure tell you about the atheist's view of the universe? What does the game of chance we just played have to do with the atheist's worldview? Do you now see why, in the opinion of the atheist, there is no such thing as fairness/unfairness in the universe?"

5. Take the same container with the twenty numbered pieces of paper and play the game again. This time let one team have three players and the other team one player. Each player draws one number (this means that one team gets three chances), and the player with the highest number wins a point for their team. The first team to accumulate three points win.

6. After the game, ask the group: "Wasn't this also a game of chance, not of skill?" Then ask the solo player: "Even though it was a game of chance, do you think that the game was fair? If you lost one thousand dollars playing this game, what would you do? Would you just accept this as bad luck and move on?"

Group Questions

Objective: To examine how atheists tend to act as if some things are fair/unfair and right/wrong

1. Look at Figures 32 and 34. In what ways are atheists being inconsistent and hypocritical? The author reminds us that Lenin and Stalin were atheists. Did they accept everything in life as 100% chance or did they act as if there were injustices to correct?
2. Look at Figures 29 and 30. Do you agree or disagree with the author that everyone, including the atheist, acts as if some things are unfair? (Write on the board: "Point One: Everyone acts as if the universe is unfair.")
3. Look at Figure 31. What is the main point of this figure? (Write on the board: "Point Two: Everyone must admit that fairness also exists.")
4. Look at Figure 35. What is the main point of this figure? (Write on the board: "Point Three: The atheist is no exception.")

Group Study

Objective: To understand that justice (fairness) and morality (right) must come from God

1. Have the group name some things that would be considered unjust/wrong, no matter the situation. List these on the board. Then have them name some things that would be considered just/right, no matter the situation. List these on the board.
2. Write "Thou shalt not..." beside the list of unjust/wrong actions and "Thou shalt..." beside the list of just/right actions.
3. Read Romans 2:15. Discussion: "Do you agree with Paul that there are rules planted within us concerning what is right and wrong and what is just and unjust?"
4. Study together the reading of Day 36. Discussion: "If rules of morality and justice exist, did they come from nature or from something above nature?" (Write on the board: "Point Four: The

rules of justice and morality cannot exist unless God exists.")

5. Read Day 37 together as a review of sessions three and four.

Group Homework

Objective: To encourage individual preparation for Session Five

1. Read "the *Argument from Supernatural Belief*" (Days 38-45).

2. Write down any questions or comments as you read.

3. Write a fictional short story, less than one page in length, with at least two original characters in the plot.

Session Five: the *Argument from Supernatural Belief* (Days 38-45)

Group Questions

Objective: To explain why humanity's supernatural belief must have a supernatural origin

1. Consider the blind man in Figure 38. How could this man, trapped in darkness, begin to believe that light exists? Could he come to this belief on his own, without outside help?

2. Look at Figure 39. How could the cave fish, trapped in darkness, become aware of light? How could the ocean-bottom fish, trapped miles below, become aware of the ocean surface? Could they come to this awareness on their own, without outside help?

3. According to Figure 40, what do atheists consider to be 100% reality. (Write on the board: "Atheism: Man is engulfed by nature." Then draw a circle around a stick-man to show how, according to atheists, man is totally trapped within nature.) How could this man, totally trapped in nature, begin to believe that a world other than nature (a supernatural world) exists? Could he come to this awareness on his own, without outside help?

4. According to Figure 42, both atheists and theists agree that humans have always tended to believe in the supernatural. The atheist states that this supernatural belief came from nature itself. What problems do you see with this theory?

Group Activity

Objective: To examine how humanity's belief in God implies His existence

1. Ask a couple of group members to read the short stories they were assigned as homework. As they read their stories, write on the board the characters' names. If no short stories are ready, give the group

five minutes to write a fifty-word short story and then choose two to be read aloud. Write down the names of the characters of the stories as they are read.

2. After the stories have been read, ask the group: "Are these characters aware of anything outside the storyline?" Ask the authors of the short stories: "Do these characters have any idea that you exist or the room where you wrote the story exists? Is there any way, without outside help, for them to become aware of you and your world?"

3. Ask the group to add a few words to their stories that would make these characters aware of the author's existence. Then ask: "Could the characters have ever come to know that their author/creator existed without outside help?"

4. Refer the group to Figure 43. Ask: "What does this tell us about the origin of our supernatural belief? Is it possible for us to be aware of a world beyond nature and of a supernatural God who created us unless God acted to make us aware?"

Group Study

Objective: To emphasize God's active role in humanity's supernatural awareness

1. Read Psalm 100, then look at Figure 41. If the world is so bad, as atheists claim, isn't it odd that humans, like the psalmist, have come to believe that God is good?

2. Look at Figure 44. Now read Hebrews 1:1,2. Do these verses imply, like the figure, that God over many centuries and through many avenues has been teaching humanity the truth about Him? Who does the writer of Hebrews proclaim to be the ultimate expression of who God is?

3. Look at Figure 45 to review where we've been and where we're going.

Group Homework

Objective: To encourage individual preparation for Session Six

1. Read "the *Argument from Human Characteristics*" (Days 46-51).
2. Write down any questions or comments as you read.
3. Make a list of five positive human traits and five negative human traits.

<u>Session Six</u>: the *Argument from Human Characteristics* (Days 46-51)

<u>Group Activity</u>

Objective: To show how an article's characteristics demand a source consistent with them

1. Before the session, put the following items in three shoe boxes (labeled Box 1, Box 2, and Box 3):

    *Box 1- a safety pin, a sheet of paper, two crayons, a plastic fork, and some adhesive tape

    *Box 2- a paper clip, a bar of soap, two toothpicks, a few dried beans, and a straw

    *Box 3- a birthday candle, an unpeeled potato, two pennies, a piece of string, and a small pair of scissors

2. Divide the group into three teams (Team 1, Team 2, and Team 3) and give the appropriate box to each. Make sure they know to keep the identity of their articles hidden from the other teams.

3. Give the teams five minutes to construct something from the articles in the box.

4. After the five minutes of construction, have each team display its creation while the other two try to guess the five articles that were in the box. Ask the group how they were so sure the boxes contained these articles.

5. Now show the group a creation of your own (constructed before the session) that includes the following items: a large pickle, a toothbrush, two leaves, a CD, and some masking tape. Ask the group to guess the articles that were in your box at home. Then ask them what they would say if you told them that there were no leaves or masking tape in the box. Could it be possible for your creation to originate from that box alone? Why not?

6. Now refer the group to Figures 47 and 48. Ask them what the group activity and these figures have in common.

Group Questions

Objective: To show how humanity's positive characteristics demand the existence of God

1. When you look at yourself and other humans, what positive characteristics do you see?
2. Look again at Figures 47 and 48. Why doesn't the atheistic worldview make sense?
3. How would you answer the questions posed by the author in Day 47's reading?
4. Look at Figure 46. Read together the reading for that day. How does the *Argument from Human Characteristics* account for your positive characteristics?
5. Look at Figure 49. What three explanations do atheists give for these positive human characteristics? According to Day 49's reading, what are the problems with each of these explanations?
6. Look at Figure 50. According to the author, how do atheists try to evade the main issue? Why do they attempt to do so?

Group Study (Figure 51)

Objective: To show how two recent scientific discoveries agree with creationism

1. Read the first chapter of Genesis together, taking turns reading verses.
2. Discuss the ways that these verses tend to conflict with what the group was taught in high school and collegiate science courses.
3. Study together the author's explanation of two recent scientific discoveries: background radiation in the universe and the anthropic principle. (See "Endnotes, Day 51" for the author's summary of these discoveries.)
4. Discuss the ways that these discoveries tend to agree with the account in Genesis.

<u>Group Homework</u>

Objective: To encourage individual preparation for Session Seven

1. Read "the *Argument from Personal Testimony*" (Days 52-55).
2. Write down any questions or comments as you read.
3. Write your own personal testimony of the reality of God in your life.

<u>Session Seven</u>: the *Argument from Personal Testimony* (Days 52-55)

<u>Group Questions</u>

Objective: To discuss humanity's tendency throughout history to profess belief in God

1. Look at Figure 52. Is it encouraging to you that atheism has always been the minority opinion? What weakness does the author admit concerning this figure? Why does the author believe that, in this case, the majority is right?

2. Do you think that people today believe in God because they are uninformed of evidence to the contrary or that they are aware of that evidence yet continue to believe? What has the evidence presented in this book done to your faith in God?

3. According to the reading on Day 53, what five reasons do atheists usually give for not believing in God? Do you know of anyone who has argued thusly? What has been the answer of theists to each of these reasons? Which of these answers appeals to you the most?

<u>Group Activity</u>

Objective: To consider the personal testimonies of the author and group members

1. Read together the author's personal testimony on Day 54.

2. Ask group members if they would read their homework assignment to the group.

3. Discuss the effect of these testimonies. Did they seem to encourage or discourage the members of the group?

4. Refer the group to the five arguments for God's existence summarized in Day 55's reading. Ask each member to rank on a piece of paper the five arguments from their most favorite to their least favorite.

Tally the votes for each argument, list the overall rankings on the board, and discuss the results.

Group Study

Objective: To discuss the dynamic relationship between faith and doubt

1. Read the account in Mark 9:14-27 of the healing of a boy with an evil spirit.
2. Reread verse 24. What does this statement by the boy's father say about him? How did Jesus respond to this statement? What does this response say about Jesus?
3. Why do you think the author used Luke 17:5 and Mark 9:24 as the quotations preceding his personal testimony on Day 54?

Group Homework

Objective: To encourage individual preparation for Session Eight

1. Read "Closing Steps" (Days 56-60).
2. Write down any questions or comments as you read.
3. Make a list of the following:
   a. Three Bible verses that declare God's existence
   b. Two arguments in this book that have helped you the most
   c. One person you know who is not a Christian but believes in God

Session Eight: Closing Steps (Days 56-60)

Group Questions
Objective: To recognize the limitations and merits of the author's arguments for God

1. Look at Figure 56. Do you agree or disagree with the author's conscious decision to minimize Biblical references?
2. Look at Figure 57. Have you tended to embrace people of other faiths as fellow theists? How far do you think that embrace should go?
3. Look at Figure 58. What five irrefutable facts did the author use as his starting points? Do you agree that both atheists and theists would consider these five facts to be true? In your opinion, does a theistic or atheistic worldview best explain these five facts?

Group Activity
Objective: To examine how the various arguments for God's existence are related

1. Before the class begins, hide an object in the room and write five different sets of directions to it. Make sure that four contain false clues that make it impossible to find the object and one contains the right clues.
2. Distribute the five sets of directions to five group members and ask them to find the object. After it is found, explain why only one group member found the hidden object. Ask them: "Was the object's existence proven by that one set of correct directions? Was the object's existence weakened to any extent by the fact that the other directions were false?"
3. After the object hunt is over, tell the group to correctly fill in the blanks to this math problem:
   12 + 23 = ___ + 34 = ___ + 45 = ___ + 56 = ___ + 67 = ANSWER
   Ask them what would happen to the final answer if they got any of

the sums wrong along the way.

4. Refer the group to Figure 59. Discuss how the five arguments for God's existence are like the set of directions and not like the series of sums. Why is this important to the person ascending the slope of God's existence?

Group Study

Objective: To acknowledge the witness of the universe to the existence of God

1. Read together Romans 1:19-20.
2. Discuss whether God's existence can be perceived, as Paul says, by looking at the universe around us. Besides His existence, what else (if anything) do you think the universe tells us about God?

Group Homework

Objective: To encourage individual preparation for Session Nine

1. Read the "Afterword" to this book.
2. Write down any questions or comments as you read.
3. Make a list of the following:
    a. Three personal comments (positive or negative) about this book
    b. Three words that describe your faith in God
    c. Three questions about God's nature or character that you would like answered

Session Nine: Afterword

Group Questions

Objective: To critique the author's approach to the existence of God

1. In the first paragraph, the author mentions several possible criticisms of the way he has dealt with the subject of God's existence. What, in your opinion, are the book's weaknesses and strengths?
2. In the second paragraph, the author defines his intended audience. Who is that audience? Do you believe that many people inside and outside of church struggle with God's existence?

Group Activity

Objective: To analyze the tendency for one's view of God to change over time

1. Select a song for the group to listen to and, as the song plays, have the members write down their impression of the music.
2. When the song is over, ask the group members to relate their impression of the song in its initial stages. Discuss whether or not their impression changed as the music continued.
3. Ask: "Has your view of God changed over the course of your lifetime? If so, how?"
4. Discuss ways that one could describe the music objectively (such as fast, slow, loud, soft, instrumental, vocal, etc.) and ways that it could be described subjectively (such as beautiful, touching, sensitive, romantic, stimulating, etc.).
5. Discuss how faith in God can be both objective and subjective.

Group Study

Objective: To assess the effect of this book on the group

1. Read together the quote from Karen Armstrong's book.
2. Discuss the surprises you have experienced along your journey.
3. Would you or would you not recommend this book to a friend? Why or why not?

INDEX OF NAME AND SUBJECTS

135–36, 178
Sillem, Edward 35, 149
skepticism 174, 194, *also see*
     doubt
Smith, George H. 170
soul 146
Southern Baptists – *see* Baptists,
     Southern
Stalin, Joseph 106, 109, 226
Strobel, Lee 171, 190, 201–2
suffering 77-89, 116, 171, 197,
     198, 223–24
Sumer 138, 139
supernatural 18, 20, 24, 31,
     113–14, 116-17, 146, 149,
     153, 155, 156, 178, 187,
     188, 202–3, 228–29,
     – *see also* Argument from
     Supernatural Belief

T
Taylor, Richard 108
teleology 207–8
Templeton, Charles 84, 88, 171
testimony – *see* Argument from
     Personal Testimony
theism 12, 13, 33, 35, 36–37,
     39, 40, 65–67, 69, 70, 73,
     81, 111, 142, 159, 162–63,
     165–68, 170–72, 177, 185–
     85, 187–88, 195, 198
     -advantages of, 19–29, 75, 219
     -arguments for – *see* Argument
        from…
     - definition of, 7, 30–31
theology 7, 11, 32–33, 174, 192,
     198, 207–8
     -conservative, 9, 10, 12
     -moderate, 10
     -liberal 10
Trueblood, Elton 16, 88

U
unfairness – *see* injustice
universe 8, 12, 20, 26, 31, 44,
     71–73, 192, 207–8, 232,
     237
     -beginning of, 60–67, 69,
        76, 163, 201
     -design of, 47–49, 53–54,
        55, 58, 71, 81, 91, 187,
        207–8, 222
     -disorder of, 24, 29, 77-79,
        80–82, 88–89, 91, 128–
        30, 205–6, 223
     -expansion of, 204–5
     -randomness of, 24, 104–9,
        204–6
     -testimony of (about God)
        - *see* Argument from…

V
Voltaire 56, 201

W
Wells, C. Richard 7–8
Wittgenstein, Ludwig 113
worldview 18, 127, 146, 149,
     163, 179

ISBN 1-41205110-X

9 781412 051101